INDIVIDUALIZED INSTRUCTION

Teaching Strategies
Focusing
on the Learner

George Ray Musgrave · University of Houston

INDIVIDUALIZED INSTRUCTION

Teaching Strategies
Focusing
on the Learner

Allyn and Bacon, Inc. *Boston* · *London* · *Sydney*

Library of Congress Cataloging in Publication Data

Musgrave, George Ray, 1922-
  Individualized instruction.

  Includes bibliographies and index.
  1. Individualized instruction. I. Title.
LB1031.M87   371.39'4   74-26554

ISBN 0-205-04709-2 (hardbound)
ISBN 0-205-04779-3 (paperbound)

Printed in the United States of America

Contents

Preface

Everyone talks about individualized instruction. Undergraduate students preparing to teach talk about individualized instructional strategies in classes where theory and practice are usually poles apart. Graduate students attend education classes and become sophisticated talkers and writers concerning individualized instructional concepts and practices. Teachers attend local, state, and national meetings where the themes and entire programs are devoted to individualized instruction. Yet, few teachers actually practice individualized instructional strategies in their classrooms. Is it possible that teachers have been taught to talk and write about individualized instruction, while they have not been taught how to implement these practices in their classrooms?

Have you ever sat with groups of educators and listened to them define and describe individualized programs and practices? Everyone seems to espouse a different definition and description of individualized instructional programs and a different theory of how they should be implemented.

Some educators believe that an open-spaced arena is synonymous with individualized instruction. They provide the arena first, hoping that open spaces, resource centers, and team-teaching arrangements will transform teachers' attitudes and beliefs and, thus, induce them to individualize. Other educators believe that techniques such as individual machines and media, programmed materials, and content modules will result in an individualized operation. Administrators attempt various organizational designs, such as homogeneous grouping, nongraded schools, continuous progress, dual progress, the Dalton Plan, and the Winnetka Plan, all designed to eliminate nonpromotion and to promote individualized instruction. Each of these plans and techniques is a small step toward individualizing.

Educators have spent millions of dollars on in-service programs that were supposed to prepare teachers to implement definitive individualized practices with students in their classrooms. Unfortunately, these programs still followed the "talk-about/write-about" format. Regardless of which definition, which program description and design, or which organizational plan a particular school system may adopt for implementing individualized instructional practices, the individual teachers will still follow procedures that they believe are valid from day to day. They are willing to change only when the change fits their philosophy of education, and then only if they receive an in-depth experience with the change and find it successful for themselves.

Complete individualization is a goal for educators much as democracy is a goal for Americans or Christianity is a goal for Christians. Everyone in education should strive to reach the goal, knowing that complete individualization is rare, if not impossible. Anytime, however, that the school situation is focusing on the individual student in the teaching-learning process, another step is being made toward the ultimate goal.

Many books and articles have been written about the theory of individualized instruction. Numerous other books and articles have described procedures in general terms couched in educational pedagogy. So this book emphasizes actual procedures rather than merely talking about theoretical procedures. It gives step-by-step instructions for focusing on the learner, whatever the particular school situation may be. The book is a practical, concrete guide for pre-service teachers in teacher-training institutions, as well as for in-service teachers and administrators.

The methods for focusing on the learner described in this book have been helpful to scores of teachers in in-service situations. Over a period of years, and in a wide range of socioeconomic and cultural settings, each technique and each procedural step has been tested and tried on all grade levels with students in actual classroom situations.

This book describes the following procedures:

1. Student-centric teaching methods
2. Instructional formations for effective learning
3. Intra-classroom grouping procedures
4. Independent study methods

5. Procedures for handling individual differences: Practitioner-Theorist Confrontations
6. Individualized student evaluation and reporting to parents
7. Focus-on-the-learner programs

I should like to thank the University of Houston and Houston Independent School District for allowing me to conduct a three-year research project on how to focus on the learner.

Specifically, I want to acknowledge the fine support I received from Dr. Charles Nelson, Gloria Schiwetz, and teachers and administrators involved in the Ryan Project and Teaching Strategies Program. I am grateful to Shirley Smith for helping me to edit the original manuscript.

INDIVIDUALIZED INSTRUCTION

Teaching Strategies
Focusing
on the Learner

I. Student-Centric Teaching Methods

Whole-Class Discussion
Small-Group Discussion
Oral Reporting
Symposiums and Panels
Whole-Class Debates
Role-Playing and Sociodrama
Brainstorming
Small-Group Dictation
Small-Group Peer Teaching
Textbook Dramatizations
Simulations and Simulating Games
Discovery Methods
Summary

If all students learned in precisely the same manner, or if they all reacted to classroom situations in the same way, then each teacher could select those teaching methods that best fit his personality and use them over and over again as long as he teaches. Admittedly, this is the practice of many teachers, but evidence clearly indicates that students have different learning styles. No two students react to a learning situation in the same way. Therefore, teachers should have a wide repertoire of teaching methods so that they can match the appropriate strategy and technique to the particular learning style of each student.

The predominant teaching methods today are teacher-centric; that is, the focus in the teacher-learner situation is centered on the teacher. Methods that would be defined as teacher-centric include lectures, teacher demonstrations, and most recitations. Teachers must be able to conduct teacher-centric presentations in an exemplary manner, for there are times when teacher-centric methods best suit the topic, the teacher's purpose, and the nature of the lessons, as well as the students' learning preferences and styles. My premise, however, is that teacher-centric methods are practiced excessively, and student-centric methods are not used enough. When teachers practice teacher-centric methods to the extent that the teachers are the stars in the classroom, then teachers become the active participants during the teaching-learning situation while the students are passive learners until feedback time. Even then, feedback information is controlled by the teacher.

Student-centric methods focus on the learner during the teaching-learning situation. Examples of student-centric methods other than those described in Chapter 3 include whole-class discussions, small-group discussions, round-table discussions, panels, symposiums, oral reporting, role-playing, whole-class and semiformal debates, brainstorming, small-group dictation, small-group peer teaching, textbook dramatizations, simulations, and gaming situations. Student-centric methods place students in the spotlight so that they become active learners and the teacher's role becomes more diversified. Freeing the teacher from having to present all the time allows him to assume the roles of motivator, guide, evaluator, and helper to a greater extent.

The purpose of this chapter is to describe student-centric presentation methods in a way that enables teachers to use the descriptions and suggestions as a guide for developing the student-centric methods that best suit their personal teaching styles.

WHOLE-CLASS DISCUSSION

CLASSROOM SCENE 1

The instructor is in front of the room, and the students are sitting in rows facing him. The instructor talks, then asks a question. One student answers the question, and the teacher responds. Then another student answers the question, and the teacher responds. Sometimes, two or three students talk before the teacher responds. This activity continues for thirty minutes, and of the thirty-five students in the class, six students respond orally. Later, the teacher tells everyone about the class discussion that occurred in his classroom.

CLASSROOM SCENE 2

The instructor has students arranged in a large circle in the classroom, and he arranges his chair within the circle and becomes a member of the large circle group. The instructor talks and asks a question. A student responds, and the teacher waits for other students to talk, but he perceives that all eyes are on him, waiting for him to respond. Although the teacher is attempting to get the students to interact in a whole-class discussion, he is getting the same results as the instructor got in Scene One. The teacher may be facilitating instruction, but only his skills are being used effectively.

Actually, neither Scene One nor Scene Two is a description of whole-class discussion. Both describe informal recitation, which places the teacher in the starring role. Such situations occur in our schools because of misconceptions about what class discussion really is. The teachers in scenes one and two may feel good about their experiences, thinking that they have initiated a discussion. They may not recognize their serious failure to help each student become a responsible, accountable individual interacting with a group of peers through subject matter. Teachers usually have not experienced real discussions in their classes. Colleges of education have not prepared teachers to conduct real discussions, so when they fail in their attempt to use an unfamiliar whole-class discussion technique, they retreat to those practices that are familiar and seem to offer security.

If a teacher has thirty or thirty-five students in a class, the double-circle formation described in Chapter 2 is a necessity, because fruitful discussion cannot result from the interaction of that many students. A fast way to arrange students into a double-circle formation is to ask each one to choose a partner. One partner from each pair will form the inner circle, and the other partner will sit behind the first, thus forming the outer circle. The inner-circle members will discuss while the outer-circle members observe silently.

The teacher's membership in either circle will usually be detrimental to the group members and the discussion results. He should sit a small distance away from the students. But while he should be inconspicuous, he should be close enough to hear and to observe everything that goes on.

During the initial attempts at whole-class discussion, emphasis is on teaching students how to discuss through experience, so members of the inner circle choose a discussion topic that interests them. They are allowed ten minutes of uninterrupted time to discuss the topic. The teacher assigns each student in the outer circle a specific task to perform as he observes and listens to the inner-circle discussion. Tasks should be introduced gradually to accommodate the age and maturity of class members. A list of duties would include some of the following:

1. Keeping a flowchart of inner-circle participation
2. Listing the discussion roles that group members performed—that is, determining which students were initiators (questioners, idea contributors, central-issue guides, arbitrators, good summarizers, and independent thinkers) and which were goal-oriented
3. Listing outstanding contributions of group members
4. Summarizing what a particular person in the inner circle said
5. Observing and reporting body language
6. Listing the things the group members did that led toward achieving the purpose of the discussion

7. Listing things that kept the group from attaining the purpose for which it was organized
8. Checking to see if the group achieved the purpose for which it was organized

After the ten-minute time interval, both the inner- and outer-circle groups evaluate the discussion, using the outer circle's evaluation data. The teacher provides direction and input as he lists important data on a large flip chart. Later, this data may be compiled and duplicated for student information files. After the evaluative discussion, inner- and outer-circle members exchange places with their partners and repeat the entire operation.

When students gain knowledge and understanding through personal experiences, their learning is stable enough to serve as a foundation for subsequent learning. Students of all ages improve with each discussion experience until they can discuss in groups at a sophisticated level. Some students may need experience with speaking and listening exercises that facilitate keeping lines of communication open. Alternately role-playing the part of the listener, the presenter of an idea, the clarifier, and the summarizer in exemplary situations provides the instructional base from which the student operates in an increasingly expanding spiral toward maturity. During the initial training period, emphasis is placed on teaching students how to discuss. Although the teacher sees that the achievement tasks for the discussion groups are completed, he emphasizes techniques and behaviors that lead toward real discussion by students as a whole class.

Whole-class discussion can be a disappointment for teachers and students when they attempt to complete complex objectives before they learn to complete simple objectives. If the topic being discussed was crime in the streets, a worthwhile task for a group learning how to discuss would be to list the causes of crime. After students have demonstrated proficiency in group discussion while completing achievement tasks that are progressively more complex, a list of twelve or fifteen achievement task objectives can be completed during a forty-minute discussion period. For example, if students in a recreational reading program have read the same short story, it would not be unreasonable to expect them to demonstrate ten cognitive objective behaviors and five affective behaviors. An example of a cognitive behavioral objective for this lesson might be that the students will be able to describe the personality characteristics of the main characters in the

story. An example of an affective behavioral objective might
be that the students will be able to relate how they felt when
they read a particular passage in the story. An important
point to remember is that achievement task completion is an
integral part of any discussion; without it, whole-class discussion will drift into segmented conversation.

Evaluation is a necessary requirement for each discussion period. Equal time and emphasis should be placed on
evaluating socialization tasks that improve whole-class discussion as a student-centric method for teaching and evaluating achievement task objectives that make certain that
whole-class discussion is worthwhile. In addition to the
shared evaluation period previously described, individual
students should keep socialization checklist forms about
themselves. During personal conference periods, students
should have the opportunity to discuss their checklist in
relation to the checklist that the teacher keeps on each student. The achievement task evaluation should be a daily
exercise. At times, achievement task evaluation may call for
written data from students, which can be placed in their
folders. In other instances, oral responses may be best to
show the teacher which members of the class have reached
the achievement task objectives.

The whole-class discussion method can be the most
appropriate and effective teaching method in many instances; its value for a particular lesson can be determined by
the teacher's purposes and objectives, the nature of the subject matter, and the students' level of sophistication. Generally speaking, the following types of lessons may be taught
using the whole-class discussion method:

1. Sharing current events and affairs
2. Discussing controversial issues
3. Interpreting and discussing stories, poems, books, and all
   other types of literature
4. Sharing information and discussing subject-matter topics
5. Discussing school and class disciplinary rules and procedures
6. Talking about merits and demerits of mass media such as
   television shows, movies, radio, and recordings
7. Discussing topics that are relevant to the group members: sex, life and death, interpersonal relations, drug
   abuse, and tobacco smoking
8. Sharing riddles, jokes, personal stories, or imaginary experiences

9. Listening to music and discussing all aspects of the rendition

10. Reviewing any subject matter unit or topic

Whether the teacher is presenting or students are reporting, when the purpose of a particular lesson is to present information to students, media presentations are more effective than whole-class discussion.

During whole-class discussions, students are active participants in the teaching-learning process. All class members are involved, which leads to class cohesiveness and unity. Students are interested in attempting tasks that they help to plan and to evaluate. An even more important point, though, is that students are communicating and cooperating with each other in the classroom. If students were allowed to experience real discussion sessions from kindergarten through high school, communication skills and interpersonal relations would be on a higher plane.

SMALL-GROUP DISCUSSION

CLASSROOM SCENE

At the beginning of a class period, thirty-five seventh-grade students are engaged in a planning session with their government teacher. Students have been researching all aspects of the capital punishment issue, and today they have decided to debate the issue as a whole-class activity. First, teacher and students decide to work in small groups of five to share ideas and suggestions and to gain the consensus of group members concerning relevant points. A decision is made to allow the groups fifteen minutes to list as many points on each side of the question as they can.

When the teacher announces that students may break whole-group formation, students pick up their chairs and arrange themselves into seven groups in a quiet and orderly manner. Voices are low and well modulated, and a business-like atmosphere prevails as students accept group membership roles willingly so that their group will be able to finish each task on time.

The teacher moves from group to group, asking questions, making comments and suggestions, and giving aid and encouragement. If something occurs in a particular group that all should hear or note, the teacher calls "time out" and clarifies or discusses the points with students. At all times, the teacher is enthusiastic and interested in an individual student's contributions and remarks, and the teacher's manner indicates that he has high expectations based on faith in students' abilities and goal orientation.

After the fifteen minutes have expired, each student has a list of points to debate regardless of which side of the question he is asked to debate. Also, the students have discussed the points to some extent in small groups, which has helped them to refine their arguments.

On the surface, organizing and teaching students in small groups seems to be simple. However, the only reason the procedure in the illustration was simple and successful is that the teacher had taught students small-group discussion techniques. Too often, students are merely placed in small groups and acquisition of all the socialization skills and procedures is left to chance. Teachers and students are soon disorganized and discouraged, and small-group discussions are not attempted again. The teacher in the illustration above has strategies and techniques for teaching small-group discussion that would be beneficial for all teachers.

This teacher started the school term by having students engage in whole-group activities. Students learned the necessary discussion techniques in whole-class discussion groups before small-group discussion was attempted. By developing students' socialization skills and understandings in a structured setting initially, the teacher was then able to concentrate on skills and understandings that were unique to small-group participation.

Small-group discussions can easily get out of hand and become noisy. The noise level allowed for small-group participation varies from teacher to teacher. Because of certain requirements that were superimposed on this teacher, he felt that the class must maintain a low noise level so that others in the building would tolerate small-group discussion. During a whole-group discussion period concerning noise-level requirements, teacher and students decided on these procedures:

1. The teacher may buy an instrument for measuring decibels during small group discussions, and list decibel readings after the discussion period. Try to keep noise levels within an acceptable range.
2. The teacher may establish low-voice and whisper-time sessions to teach low-noise-level communication.

3. Have group members be responsible for each other to maintain a low noise level.
4. Learn to laugh in a quiet way.
5. Have a hand signal for students to indicate that the noise level is too high.
6. Play low-volume background stereo music.
7. Evaluate your group and yourself on a noise-level checklist during whole-group evaluation time.

Although these suggestions helped to make class members responsible for their behavior, the essential reason that a desirable noise level was maintained centered on the following teacher behaviors:

1. He demonstrated a low, well-modulated voice to students as he moved from group to group.
2. He moved from group to group in a quiet, businesslike manner without spending too much time with any one group.
3. He accentuated the positive by identifying class members as "the best," "improving," "good," and "better."
4. He maintained composure under stress. He did not yell "get quiet" or "shut up," nor did he use fear, ridicule, or sarcasm as disciplinary techniques.
5. He gained students' respect so that they wanted to share disciplinary responsibilities.
6. He projected a firm but friendly attitude toward students so that they spent only a minimum amount of time misbehaving.
7. He caused a "we" atmosphere to develop with class members without relinquishing his role as the teacher.
8. He projected a positive self-concept that allowed him to accept and to interact with students in a worthwhile manner.

Even when members of a small group have the socialization skills necessary for a successful discussion and know how to operate in a quiet and orderly way, a nebulous teaching-learning situation can still occur if the students are confused about the purpose and goals for small-group discussion. This teacher took the following necessary steps:

1. During daily planning sessions with students, the teacher established daily goals and objectives.
2. While groups were in session, he walked from group to group helping students to achieve the objectives.
3. By establishing time limits with students for the comple-

tion of daily tasks, he induced students to stay on the
topic until the task was completed.

4. He provided evaluation time at the close of the period so
   that students could evaluate how well they achieved the
   established objectives. Information and knowledge
   learned during small-group discussions formed an integral part of their overall evaluation; consequently, students perceived the small-group discussion time as being
   important, not merely something apart from regular
   learning tasks.

This teacher realized that small-group discussion was an
effective technique for him because students had initially
learned the discussion techniques thoroughly in a whole-
group formation. Simply because the small-group discussion
method of teaching was an effective method for him, he did
not make small-group discussions an everyday activity.

ORAL REPORTING

CLASSROOM SCENE

A student is at the front of the classroom reading from a paper
that he is holding. He has difficulty reading all the words he
has copied from the encyclopedia, which is his only source.

Students at their desks are looking out the window,
reading library books, or attempting to decipher what the
reader is saying. All dread the days to come, because each
student will stand before the class and give an oral report on
his assigned topic.

The teacher is in the back corner of the room with his
grade book, and as the student finishes his report, the teacher
places a letter grade beside the student's name. When the
student returns to his seat, the teacher calls the name of
another student, and a similar scene occurs.

This scene depicts the situation that occurs when students have been asked to make an oral report but have not
been taught how to report. This procedure is a misuse of oral
reporting as a student-centric method for teaching. What
necessary steps should a teacher take to make oral reporting
an effective teaching-learning situation?

If the purpose for oral reporting is to allow students to
research a topic and then share the information learned with
their classmates so that all will learn, then students should

be taught how to gather information. If a specific source has not been cited for the report, students should start by consulting general sources. As they skim the information, they should note sections that they will need to read carefully later. When the reading pertains specifically to their topic, they should take notes so that they can report the information in their own words. General sources usually give references that enlarge on the topic. Students should follow the same research techniques for specific readings, but to keep from including superfluous material, they should keep in mind such things as the reporting method, the time limit for reporting, and the type of information that will be most interesting to the class. After all the information has been gathered, the notes should be translated into the proper reporting form.

Research skills cannot be left to chance; they must be taught step by step. Lessons must be conducted on how to find and use general reference books; how to translate written ideas in a book into one's own words without sounding stilted or bookish; how to find and use specific sources that are pertinent to the report; and how to organize material into a meaningful report that clearly outlines and supports one central idea.

Preparation skills are just as important for children unable to read as they are for students who have learned to read. They must be taught to survey the topic as a whole; look for meaningful parts that would be interesting to classmates; and then prepare the report, sequence by sequence, in their minds. For example, a group of kindergarten children who visited the zoo are asked to prepare a report on the animal that was most interesting to them. First, they must collect data from their memory bank, other students, family and friends, pictures from books, and teacher input. Next, they must be taught to consider which things are interesting and important. Then they should learn to make a mental outline of the things they are going to say in their report. Practicing the report and receiving feedback at home is a final preparatory step that is beneficial for all students who have supportive home environments.

After the research skills have been taught, students should receive lessons on reporting techniques and skills before actually reporting to others. If they plan to read their report, they should receive instructions on how to read to an audience. Taking television and radio announcers as models, students should practice reading sentences, then report these sentences to an audience in conversational tones while looking at different individuals in the audience. One of the most effective techniques for teaching students to read to an audience is to have a student play the role of a television or radio announcer, reporting news stories to others while using the proper skills and techniques.

Students who talk from a mental or written outline should incorporate many of the memorization techniques that students use when they memorize their entire report. Even though an outline is very useful for forming a framework for the report, it takes more than a good outline to ensure a fluent delivery. If students do not practice delivering the information, the report will lack conciseness. To have to glance at their notes too often minimizes the effectiveness of a report. The reporting techniques are similar, then, for students who memorize their reports or talk from an outline. The reporter should use his own words. His eye contact should move from student to student, but he should be careful not to shift eye contact too fast or remain with one student too long. Nonverbal language and voice intonation should be pleasant to the listener while matching the personality of the reporter. Being able to see and hear themselves on tape recorders and videotape recorders can help students to improve their presentation. Allowing students to make short oral reports often and in various situations where they can be successful improves their speaking techniques, and each time they see themselves as being capable, their poise, confidence, and self-image as a speaker improves.

A limited number of students in each class have the ability to make a report interesting and meaningful without props; however, almost every reporter can improve his report by using supportive media. But before students can use supportive media for oral reporting, they need specific lessons that teach the necessary skills. For example, if a student intends to use the chalkboard to support his report, he must know that the charts, diagrams, key thoughts, or even questions for discussion should be placed on the chalkboard before he starts reporting. If he intends to use pictures, he should choose pictures that are large enough to be seen by everyone, and he should place them on a standard high enough for everyone to see. He must learn not to pass out pictures to students while he is giving his report, for if he does, he will lose the attention of the class members who are looking at the pictures. Students should be taught to use the overhead projector, the slide projector, tape recorders, and other machines that may be available. Flannel boards, puppets, and flip-boards are props that can make oral reports more interesting to students. The skills needed for effective use of props must be demonstrated for students, and then they must have experiences using props to support and to supplement oral reports.

The teacher also has critical teaching responsibilities while the students are preparing their reports. The teacher should be able to have personal conferences with students who are preparing reports, because only three or four are preparing reports at the same time. Usually, these reports are complementary, so they can be presented at a symposium. All students should have a chance to report, but the reports should be spaced so that monotony and repetition will not have to be endured. Working with three or four students enables the teacher to help students with their research, presentation mode, and selection of supportive media. If a student is reporting for the first time, a private practice session may be valuable, depending on the student's abilities and desires. The goal for both teacher and student is a report that gives information to classmates in a meaningful and interesting manner. When a student does a good job of reporting, the teacher and students can point out the practices and techniques that they thought made the report interesting and meaningful.

Methods and techniques for oral reporting are learned through observation. Teachers have opportunities and responsibilities to model the best oral reporting techniques as they present lessons during the school day. Just as students are expected to remember the material presented in oral reports by the teacher, they should also be expected to remember the content of the reports of other students.

Finally, as a whole-class project, students may design a checklist, or rating scale, of oral reporting items. After a reporting experience, students can rate themselves and then discuss the ratings during a personal conference with the teacher. As the student discusses each item and compares his rating with the teacher's rating, the student and teacher are usually able to assimilate opinions and reach a consensus.

Grading reports on a comparative basis is impossible. If the goal of oral reporting is to give other class members knowledge and understandings while giving the reporter the experience of organizing and planning and presenting an oral report, then each student must be taught as an individual. This means accepting him as he is and where he is and helping him to improve. When the student reaches a personal goal, regardless of how that goal relates to the goals of others, he should be rewarded. The use of comparative marks conflicts with the above stated philosophy and is detrimental to students' learning, for it hinders growth.

One class devised the rating scale for evaluating oral reports shown in Figure 1.1.

Lesson Ideas for Teaching Oral Reporting Skills

Collect sets of reference books, encyclopedias, almanacs, book and magazine digests, or any other general reference work series available. Divide students into small groups and let them find a topic as you name it. If students have difficulty, instruct all the students in ways to find the topic quickly. Later, groups may wish to compete with other groups. Give each group a list of fifteen topics and allow groups to compete on the bases of speed and accuracy.

After a teacher demonstration on the use of the card catalog in the library, assign students lists of topics and help them to find specific reading references for their topic. Guide students step by step to be sure they can use the card catalog to find material. Encourage systematic, consistent organization by teaching the students how to arrange the collected data on cards or in notebooks. Organization may follow alphabetical, chronological or sequential order to make maximum use of the student's time with resource materials.

Initially, teach students to arrange notes in their own words by giving them short paragraphs from general references. Allow a student to read his paragraph to the other students and then have him repeat the content in his own words.

Demonstrate proper oral reporting techniques while using the chalkboard as a prop, and allow students to critique the presentation.

To help students learn how to operate various props while reporting, divide the class into small groups. Each student should experience each type of prop at least once in a small group before he is asked to report to the whole group. Peer-group feedback sessions can help the reporter if students have been taught to critique positively, not derogatorily.

DATE _November 25, 1975_ NAME _Jane Doe_

1 outstanding	3 satisfactory
2 above average	4 needs improvement

Research:

1. Collected important information   1   2   ③   4
2. Translated notes into own words   1   2   ③   4
3. Organized material into reporting form   1   2   3   ④
4. Practiced report prior to reporting   1   ②   3   4
5. Used more than one source of information   1   2   3   ④

Reporting:

1. Spoke in clear conversational tones   1   2   ③   4
2. Spoke in own words   1   2   ③   4
3. Maintained eye contact with audience   1   2   3   ④
4. Used props that fit the presentation   1   2   3   ④
5. Used props correctly   1   2   3   ④
6. Presented pertinent information   1   2   ③   4
7. Non-verbal communication was effective   1   2   ③   4
8. Handled discussion questions well   1   2   ③   4
9. Students listened carefully to report   1   2   3   ④

FIGURE 1.1 Oral Report Rating Scale

SYMPOSIUMS AND PANELS

Symposiums and panel discussions are expanded oral reporting situations. A symposium includes a number of reporters speaking individually in succession, usually reporting on different phases of the same topic. Members of the symposium are each given a time limit for reporting so that the entire program will not be too long. After the presentations have been completed, class members are allowed to question the reporters and comment on the content of the symposium.

The panel discussion is a more informal method for reporting to others. Members of the panel have researched topics that fit into an overall scheme. A moderator sets the stage for the discussion by introducing the topic and the panel members. In his introduction, the moderator explains the research areas of each panel member. Then he starts the discussion by asking a panel member a question. In an informal manner, the members of the panel enter into the discussion to present their research and viewpoints. Because the panel members do not talk in sequence, the moderator must balance panel-member input so that the panel discussion goals are met. Later, class members may present information, express views, and enter into the discussion summary.

If students have learned oral reporting skills and have learned to discuss topics as whole-group and small-group participants, then they have learned many of the individual skills that make symposiums and panel presentations successful. Still, there are additional skills that are unique to symposiums and panel presentations, and these skills must be learned before students attempt to present topics using the symposium and panel format.

Whereas previous reporting experiences for students were individual enterprises, symposiums and panels require students to become team members during the planning, researching, and reporting phases. For a symposium, all the symposium members should be involved in the selection of each member's topics. Then, as individual members research their own topics, they should note references and material that would be valuable to teammates. Team members should share and discuss research notes after each trip to the library. Final preparatory steps include completing individual reports, presenting reports to team members and receiving feedback, choosing a symposium coordinator, and deciding on the reporting design and sequence.

A symposium is really a teacher-aide group. A small group of students is helping the teacher present pertinent information to class members. So when students prepare and present symposiums for the first time, the teacher should serve as a team leader in every sense of the word. Each time the team meets, the teacher should be present to offer suggestions and advice, to ask questions, to help students select and find research sources, to resolve interpersonal issues and problems of team members, to listen to individual reports and give relevant feedback, and to help plan the symposium presentation. After the presentation, the teacher should be with the syposium team members as they evaluate the effectiveness of the presentation during an informal discussion period. If the team members wish to solicit peer feedback, they may pass out forms that ask students to list bouquets, brickbats, and suggestions. Students' names or any other identification marks should not be solicited. These reports are valuable during evaluation time (if the teacher views peer evaluations in light of tendencies and not in light of extremes).

Preparation for reporting using the panel-discussion format differs slightly from preparation for the symposium format. Panel-discussion members not only need to have comprehensive understandings about all phases of the topic to be discussed, they also need expertise in a specific area of the broad topic. Consequently, students research the broad topic first; then, after two or three informal sharing and discussion periods, each member chooses a specific area of responsibility. Each student should keep in mind as he researches his special area that anything he learns meanwhile about the broad topic will make him a more valuable member of the panel. Frequent sharing and informal discussion periods aid the panel members in choosing a moderator. Instead of preparing and practicing a three- to five-minute talk, as one does for a symposium, students must prepare a list of important points and short excerpts about their topic so that as the flow shifts from subtopic to subtopic within the framework of the overall topic, they can continue to contribute to the panel. The final sharing and discussion session can be a dress rehearsal for the actual presentation.

The skill of the moderator is the key to success. After he introduces the topic and the panel members, he must allow each panel member to submit his best points. At the same time, the moderator must make sure that the conversation flows smoothly from one member to another. The moderator has to satisfy the ego needs of panel members while seeing to it that the goals for which the panel was formed are met. At the close of the presentation, the moderator should summarize the discussion points. The best instruments for evaluating panel discussions are audiotapes and videotapes. Hearing and seeing themselves during their actual presentations and critiquing the presentation with the teacher and group members can be valuable experiences for the panel members, helping them to improve their technique.

WHOLE-CLASS DEBATES

CLASSROOM SCENE

Two groups of students, twelve in each group, are arranged so that the members of one group are facing the members of the other group. The teacher is standing at the head of the corridor that separates the two groups. The teacher calls on one student who has raised his hand. The student rises from his chair and makes three debate points for his side of the question. The debate moves from side to side as students rise to refute the opponents' points and to score points for their side of the question. The teacher is the referee, designating who speaks, how long the speaker talks, and in other ways interpreting and enforcing the rules of the debate. After fifteen minutes, he summarizes the points for both sides and concludes the debate.

The teacher of this class did a number of things to make whole-class debates meaningful and interesting for students who were learning to take a side and to debate an issue intellectually.

The whole class watched filmed debates and listed the points that were based on intellect and fortified with valid information. Then they watched the same debates to list points that were based primarily on emotion, especially when the emotions caused the speaker to present false or unreliable information.

Individually, students researched both sides of an issue. Doing that helped the students to understand that there are many points to consider on both sides of a controversial issue. Researching both sides also helped the students to have reliable data with which to refute points made by the opposition during an actual debate. Sharing and discussing research points in small groups provided students with opportunities to collect additional data and to test the validity of their arguments in a nonthreatening environment.

Before attempting a whole-class debate for the first time, the teacher conducted a teacher-student planning session to construct the roles and behaviors for the debate. Class members presented ideas, which were discussed by students and teacher until a consensus was reached. If class consensus concerning a point was positive, the teacher listed it on a flip-board. Later, the entire list of points was taken from the flip-board and duplicated, and each student received a copy.

During the debate, students raised their hands when they wished to speak, and the teacher called on as many different speakers as possible without allowing the debate to lose its impetus. After a period of time had elapsed, students could change sides and debate the opposing views if they wished. The teacher's enthusiasm and the way he enforced the rules of the debate helped to make the experience meaningful and interesting to students.

A taped playback of the debate proved to be an excellent evaluative instrument. Students were able to evaluate the debate as a group by listing the points made, weighing them on a scale of one to five, and then discussing the weighing criteria. Criteria lists became individual checklists for students' self-evaluation.

ROLE-PLAYING AND SOCIODRAMA

CLASSROOM SCENE 1

Members of a fourth-grade class have been studying an article entitled, "Getting Along With Each Other." Today, the teacher has helped a group of four students to present a staged sociodrama. Two of the four students are sitting on the teacher's desk, which has been decorated to look like a large cloud. The chalkboard, which is directly behind the desk, has been colored blue with white areas to provide a sky backdrop for the desk scene. One student wears a sign that reads "Martin Luther King." The other student is wearing a sign signaling that he is playing the role of Abraham Lincoln. As they look down on the world from their sky perch, they talk about race relations from the point of view of Martin Luther King and Abraham Lincoln. After the first two role players have depicted the beliefs of King and Lincoln, the other two sociodrama participants enter the scene, playing the parts of Malcolm X and George Wallace. Eventually, the class members ask questions, make comments, and conduct an informal conversation.

CLASSROOM SCENE 2

Members of an eleventh-grade English class have been studying the dialects spoken in the United States. Today, the students enter the classroom and stroll over to a table to select placards to display across their chests. Printed on each placard is a role to be played that requires the speaker to use a specific dialect: for example, Mississippi Delta Minister's Wife, Mexican American Farm Worker from South Texas, Black Businessman from Alabama, Cajun Musician from Louisiana, Professor from Harvard, Hippie Student from California, Baseball Fan for New York Mets, Black Television Announcer from Boston, Coal Miner from North Carolina, and Kentucky Farmer.

During a whole-class sociodrama scene, students pretend that they are attending a national meeting to formulate a standard dialect for everyone in America. Each speaker expresses views consistent with the role he is playing, speaking the dialect appropriate for the role. At the close of this meeting, a list of recommendations is to be presented to a governmental agency.

Students play their roles beautifully while speaking the correct dialect for their characterizations. After forty-five minutes of role-playing, class members recommend that the committee be disbanded, because a standardization of dialects would be impossible to accomplish and detrimental to the people.

A sociodrama is a student-centric method of teaching whereby students create or recreate situations concerning human relations, displaying the emotions appropriate to their roles. Students' attitudes and beliefs are formed from their experiences in life situations during their formative years. A sociodrama allows students to experience situations and to interact with others about the experience, thus internalizing it. Students become active participants in relevant situations that motivate them to learn more about themselves and the attitudes and beliefs of others.

Whether a teacher plans to engage a teacher-aide group to present a staged sociodrama or he plans to involve the whole class, he must give meticulous attention to the preparation, discussion, and evaluation phases of the lesson.

Preparation for a sociodrama includes helping group members with research resources and techniques and helping students to prepare necessary equipment and materials for the sociodrama. Students must be able to represent the characterization in such a way that the conversation is spontaneous and impromptu. Still, the presentation must be structured enough so that the characters and situations are accurately presented.

After the students have disengaged themselves from their roles, the teacher must be able to encourage free-flowing discourse among students. The teacher should be involved in the discourse to clarify points, to arbitrate differences, and to referee the interaction process. But he should practice discretion when stating opinions and beliefs. Too much teacher input can be detrimental to free discourse and affect student participation.

A good practice to follow before attempting a whole-class sociodrama is to conduct a staged sociodrama involving a few students and then allow the class to evaluate it. Listing relevant points on a flip-board, solicit student input concerning those things that made the sociodrama a successful learning experience for them. Next, encourage the students to develop a list of ways to improve the sociodrama. Edit and transform these lists into a goals checklist for student evaluative purposes.

Whole-class sociodrama is usually less structured than a staged sociodrama and requires less preparation time by students. This is especially true because time need not be spent preparing a presentation. But the acquisition and preparation of needed equipment and materials before the sociodrama presentation is essential to its success. The teaching plan should include a means for evaluating both the content of the sociodrama and the students' participation in it.

Evaluation of the whole-class sociodrama by students and teacher is necessary if techniques are to improve. Following the sociodrama experience, students may be divided into small problem-solving groups to list the strengths and weaknesses of the sociodrama experience. As the small groups report their opinions, relevant points can be compiled and edited, and a copy can be prepared for each student in class. Self-evaluative checklists and forms should be completed so that individual members can confer with the teacher at a specified time.

BRAINSTORMING

CLASSROOM SCENE 1

A tenth-grade creative writing class of twenty-four students has been divided into two equal groups. The teacher had previously conducted oral exercises designed to assess students' abilities to produce original and spontaneous ideas. For this particular session, students who have demonstrated competencies for producing original and spontaneous ideas orally are distributed proportionately to each group, because although only one group is presently brainstorming, the other group will assume the brainstorming responsibilities when group tasks are rotated.

The brainstorming group is arranged in a stack formation facing the teacher, who is serving as a group leader for the session. The second group is in a semicircle formation behind and to the right of the teacher, facing the brainstorming group. Large sheets of butcher paper and felt-tip markers have been placed in front of each member.

As the brainstorming group contributes ideas toward solving the problem, members of the other group use the butcher paper to record the ideas.

The problem is how to provide interesting and successful experiences and rewards for creative students who are not interested in present extracurricular activities. Group members submit ideas in rapid-fire order, and the teacher accepts each contribution, avoiding any type of nonverbal or verbal criticism or analysis. The recording group has been assigned to record individual contributions on a one-to-one basis, and recording-group members feel as though they are sharing the contributions. During the twenty-minute session, many excellent ideas are recorded:

> *"We should ask for classes designed especially for creative students."*

> *"Provide teachers with special literature about creativity and the creative student."*

> *"How about art exhibits?"*

> *"Why not have a special class for song writers?"*

> *"Could we form a club to sing songs we write?"*

> *"Why not have a special choir, with uniforms, taking trips, singing songs we write?"*

> *"Set up awards for poetry, short stories, photography presentations, artists' exhibits, . . ."*

> *"Allow students to pursue creative interests for pay in the community during part of the school day as in other work-study programs."*

*"Allow brainstorming sessions among faculty, adminis-
tration, and students concerning this topic."*

"Make nature study a part of the curriculum."

After the twenty minutes expire, the recording-group
members tape all contributions on a convenient wall for all
members of the class to observe. Items are discussed, edited,
and combined, and a final list of feasible ideas is submitted
for possible implementation. Before the period ends, the
teacher explains to the students that in the next session of
the class, following a discussion of ways to improve brainstorming sessions, the groups will exchange roles and duties
and brainstorm another problem.

CLASSROOM SCENE 2

A junior high school in a large city has a problem with
students and ex-students who loiter and roam in the halls
during class periods. The problem is so severe that teachers
lock their classroom doors when the tardy bell rings to prevent students in the halls from harassing teachers and students in classes. Security guards and administrators have
attempted to stop hall traffic during class periods, but their
efforts have not solved the problem.

During a general-assembly period, the problem is presented to all segments of the school population, including
administrators, security guards, faculty, students, auxiliary
personnel, and parents. The people are seated in six sections
of the auditorium, and the seating arrangement ensures that
all segments of the population are represented in each section. Six group leaders, plus three student recorders for each
leader, have been selected and trained to lead a thirty-minute
brainstorming session. One hundred participants have been
assigned to each group leader.

The leader of the large-group assembly explains the
problem, and five leaders of the student body give short talks
concerning the seriousness and urgency of the problem. The
assembly leader asks the audience for group cohesiveness
and support as they all work together in a brainstorming
session seeking solutions to the problem.

A popular teacher from the English department explains that brainstorming is an activity during which ideas
are expressed to a group leader in rapid-fire order without
any discussion, criticism, or analysis. The teacher explains

the rules and the procedures for the brainstorming session as follows:

1. Any serious idea that may lead to solution of the problem is acceptable.
2. There will be competition among groups and an award will be given to the group that produces the most ideas related to the topic.
3. Related ideas are acceptable as long as they build or modify the original idea.
4. Everyone should concentrate on possible solutions. Your idea may be the answer everyone is seeking.
5. State ideas precisely, quickly, and clearly.
6. Do not discuss ideas.
7. Do not criticize ideas in any way.
8. Do not attempt to analyze or evaluate ideas.
9. The session will be terminated in thirty minutes.
10. Do not begin until a signal to start is given to all groups.

Before the starting signal is given, section group leaders with microphones explain that they will recognize individuals with contributions as quickly as possible, and that they will repeat each suggestion for all to hear. The idea will be projected on the large wall by student recorders using overhead projectors so that everyone in the section can see it.

The signal to start is given, and the first participant in each of the six sections of the auditorium begins speaking. Group leaders move about among the participants to assure that all members have opportunities to express ideas. Section group leaders are enthusiastic and accepting as they give equal emphasis to each contribution. Student recorders are organized and efficient as they record each idea and project it on the wall. The signal that the thirty-minute session has ended brings moans from the audience, because the time has passed all too soon.

The assembly leader explains that section ideas will be counted and a winner will be announced in a general assembly during the next week. A committee composed of students, faculty, auxiliary personnel, security guards, parents, and administrators will be elected to compile, edit, tabulate, and evaluate ideas. A final list of ideas will be presented to everyone for approval at the earliest possible date. Another brainstorming session concerning the problem of improving general-assembly brainstorming sessions will be conducted in the near future.

Because so many ideas were submitted, the selected committee devised selection criteria. Some of the most useful ideas were:

"Select combination student-faculty patrols."

"Seek government funds for television cameras in the halls."

"Get tough on drug pushers and drug users at school."

"Let students evaluate classes for interest and utility."

"Give more recognition to students who attend classes."

"Everyone become hall-empty conscious."

"Establish more work-study programs for students who are not interested in school curriculum."

"Arrange times and suitable places for students to get together during the school day."

"Establish cooperative disciplinary policies, including students, parents, administrators, and security guards."

"Prepare a get-tough policy concerning hall behavior, and everyone help to enforce the policy."

"Make participation in academics as rewarding as participation in athletics."

"Establish a Pride Clothing Store with unique, reasonably priced clothes that identify students from our school."

"This clothing store idea could be a cooperative store that would be established and operated by our school."

The committee realized that students roaming the halls was actually a symptom of more difficult problems. Reasonable short-term ideas were implemented immediately, while many long-range ideas were initiated, and they proved to be worthwhile at a later date.

CLASSROOM SCENE 3

A class of twenty-four third-grade students has received instruction concerning the definition, purposes, and procedures for brainstorming. The whole group has practiced brainstorming techniques and evaluated its performance during the past three weeks.

Today, the class has been divided into eight small groups of three students. Each group has a special location, and newsprint and felt pens are provided at each location. The location for each group is designated by the teacher. She explains that she will give the signal for students to move into small-group formations and that they should move quietly into the location during a whisper count of three.

As soon as students are settled at their locations, the teacher explains that two students in each group will be brainstorming participants, while the third student will be a recorder. After participant and recorder roles are divided among group members, "What We Can Do About the Energy Crisis" is introduced as the topic for a fifteen-minute brainstorming session by each small group.

A signal is given to proceed, and a businesslike hum of voices indicates that individuals are contributing ideas. As the teacher walks from group to group, she nods her head to indicate approval. Occasionally, she injects an idea, restates the focus of the session, or provides positive reinforcement to groups and individuals. The teacher's enthusiasm permeates the classroom atmosphere as students seem to model her personality and behavioral characteristics.

When the brainstorming operation is concluded, recorders report ideas as the teacher and students compile, edit, criticize, and assign priorities to a list of ideas. The final list contains these ideas:

"Talk to mothers and fathers about energy crisis."

"Turn off lights when leaving my room."

"Walk or ride bicycles to school."

"Walk or ride bicycles to do errands at home."

"Do not ask mothers and fathers to take unnecessary trips."

"Wear warm clothing to school so that classroom heat will not have to be as high."

"Talk to others about ways to conserve energy."

"Do not watch television unless the program is interesting."

During a follow-up activity, this class evaluated the brainstorming session. Using a flip-board, the teacher directed a teacher-student lesson on ways to improve brainstorming sessions. A student committee helped the teacher to compile, analyze, and edit the list of suggestions. The final suggestion list was used to formulate evaluative checklist items for individual teacher-student conferences.

These public school scenes illustrate that brainstorming is appropriate for both small and large groups. In each instance, students presented ideas for solving a particular problem in which they had special insight and interest. In each case, ideas had to be presented without discussion, criticism, or analysis, and follow-up procedures for implementing valid ideas culminated each session. Students learned how to refine their brainstorming competencies by first evaluating group and individual performances and then setting improvement goals for future brainstorming sessions.

Brainstorming is a student-centric method that is especially appropriate for dealing with a problem in a direct way. Students are stimulated to think and to provide ideas in a group setting. The ability to express ideas individually to a group using brainstorming techniques has tremendous carry-over value for students in future life situations.

SMALL-GROUP DICTATION

CLASSROOM SCENE 1

A creative writing class of twenty students has been divided into five small groups. On the basis of a series of creative writing exercises developed by Getzels and Jackson,* the teacher has assessed the students' creative thinking and writing abilities. For this small-group composition lesson, polar grouping procedures are used so that each group has both students with creative writing abilities and students lacking creative writing abilities.

The students have been studying Japanese haiku. They have participated in a symposium to report on the background and history of the poetry. Students have listened to recordings of haiku and have individually explored many anthologies of the evocative art form.

Today they are composing the three-line verses as a whole-class enterprise. Initially, members of each small group reach a consensus concerning their nomination for the first line of the haiku. A spokesman for each group dictates his

* Jacob W. Getzels and Phillip W. Jackson, *Creativity and Intelligence* (New York: John Wiley and Sons, 1962).

group's choice, and the teacher records each contribution on the chalkboard. The nominations are read aloud, and students discuss and critique them. Eventually, a first line is chosen on the basis of which line most of the class members prefer, and this line becomes the first line for all groups. The procedure is repeated for the second and third lines, and the class has composed a model haiku. Later, each small group composes a complete haiku on butcher paper to be displayed on a designated section of the classroom wall for everyone to read.

The small-group dictation lesson served as a motivating springboard for a variety of individual endeavors. Class members composed and sent verses to each other, wrote and illustrated books of haiku, and published poems in the school paper. They formed a haiku correspondence club, and they wrote and received poems from a school group in Japan.

CLASSROOM SCENE 2

The fifteen students in a Spanish class have been placed in five problem-solving groups of three. During the past weeks, they have been translating stories from English to Spanish. Today's lesson is a small-group dictation exercise in which students will compose a story in Spanish as a whole-class enterprise.

First, each small group reaches a consensus regarding a title for the story. A spokesman dictates his group's nomination in Spanish to the teacher, and she records each nomination on the chalkboard. Any error in syntax or pronunciation is corrected by other group members. After all nominations have been written on the chalkboard, group spokesmen translate their titles to English. Teacher-directed choral reading of all the contributions precedes student voting on one title choice. The preferred title is placed on the center chalkboard, and the remaining titles are erased. This procedure is repeated, sentence by sentence, and after thirty minutes, a class short story has been written.

To culminate the lesson, the teacher directs the class as they read the composition in unison, first speaking Spanish, then translating their story into English. To evaluate individual student learning, the teacher gives each student an English or Spanish version of the story and has him translate it.

CLASSROOM SCENE 3

The twenty students of this second-grade class have learned whole-class discussion techniques, and they have been solving simple problems in small groups. These experiences have prepared students for small-group dictation experiences.

Today, emphasis is placed on group consensus as a requisite for writing a class story. During the whole-group formation, procedures for writing a class story are described by the teacher. First, each student in the small group will contribute a title for the story, then the group must decide which title they wish to present as their small-group choice. They will want to present their best contribution so that their title will have a chance to be the title chosen by the whole class, because after titles are nominated, one will become the title for all. A short story will be written as small groups nominate sentences for a story following the same procedures that were used to select a title. In each group, one member must not dominate other group members. Everyone must have a chance to nominate, and the final group selection must be fair.

On a whisper count of three, class members move to their designated groups. As the teacher moves from group to group, she observes that in one group a leader has emerged, and he is calling on each member of the group for a contribution before deciding which is the best title. In another group, each student in turn has been allowed to make a contribution or pass. The members have discussed the nominations, and now they are voting on the preferred group contribution. Another group is experiencing difficulty reaching a group decision. The teacher calls "time out" and talks briefly to the whole class about organizational procedures for reaching a group decision.

The teacher moves among the groups, listening, providing positive reinforcement, and, occasionally, asking questions or making comments. During the dictation period, she is a recorder, discussion leader, and teacher of processes involved in reaching a consensus. She explains that students should reach a consensus by setting up informal criteria and then analyzing each contribution according to the standards. The teacher realizes that the process is time consuming, but reaching group consensus is a valuable democratic process. Sometimes, student voting is necessary, but voting may result in a loss of enthusiasm by those students who did not vote for the elected contribution.

The teacher records dictation at the chalkboard, allowing students to spell words, punctuate sentences, and compose the story in their own words. The teacher's nonverbal behavior helps her direct and channel the composition in the right direction. She pauses, lifts her eyebrows, purses her lips, smiles, uses her hands, and changes her body posture to communicate meaning to students.

After the story is completed, the whole group reads it, chorally. Different groups read parts of the story, and eventually, individual students read designated words and sentences. Students seem to enjoy reading a story that they have composed.

An evaluative session is conducted on achievement and socialization tasks for small-group dictation. Ten students list all the ways the class might improve the story they have written, and the remaining ten students list ways consensus decision-making can be improved. Lists are compiled and edited, and copies are provided for teacher files and student notebooks.

Small-group dictation is a student-centric method that is appropriate for all subjects. These selected scenes depict classes that are composing original compositions, but small-group dictation is also applicable for solving problems in sequential steps. For example, to solve a mathematics problem, small groups may nominate initial procedures. After the teacher places each group's nomination on the chalkboard, the initial procedure for the whole class is determined by consensus. This procedure is repeated for each step until the problem is computed. Similarly, demonstrations in science, procedures in homemaking skills, compositions in music, or problems in government are appropriate areas for small-group dictation.

Small-group dictation offers these advantages for student learning:

Students are producers of learning rather than receptacles for information.

Interpersonal relationships are enhanced because while individuals are responsible for small-group products, the small group is responsible for its members.

Students experience consensus decision-making, and as they

live the process in a classroom setting, they become believers in consensus as a valid democratic process.

Small-group dictation motivates students to produce a similar product independently.

Students are held responsible for their own learning, rather than the teacher being held responsible for their learning.

Students and groups evaluate themselves according to task-oriented objectives.

Small-group dictation is an indirective method, and, of course, the method is more adaptable to indirective students and teachers. However, a directive teacher may want to use the method for variety, and the results may cause the directive teacher to establish a balance between directiveness and indirectiveness.

SMALL-GROUP PEER TEACHING

CLASSROOM SCENE 1

Thirty students in a high school Biology class were asked to fill out a questionnaire concerning lecture classes and laboratory classes. Students reported that while laboratory classes were interesting and informative, lecture sessions were repetitive and boring. On the basis of student reports, the instructor decided to experiment with student-centric methods as an alternative to lecturing. One type she chose was small-group peer teaching. Small-group peer teaching seemed to be an appropriate method for teacher and students.

In each of her classes, the teacher placed students in small groups of equal number. Each group was an autonomous unit formed to demonstrate concepts to members of that group. Teaching centers with the necessary materials for special lessons were arranged in the room. Lesson plans included objectives for the demonstration stated in learner terms, subject matter, suggestions and presentation procedures, and sample post-test problems for student members of each group.

For example, a class of thirty students is divided into six groups of equal number. The instructor prepares five demonstration lessons and post-test questions for each lesson. One student in each group receives the first demonstration plan three days before the actual lesson. Student Two receives a demonstration plan one day later, and the procedure is repeated until each student has received a demonstration lesson plan. The peer teaching operation begins three days later, and students in each group present a different demonstration on consecutive days until everyone in the small group has presented a demonstration lesson. Demonstrations are evaluated on the basis of performance criteria that class members have prepared and on the basis of student learning as measured by objective post-test items.

On this particular day, the first student in each group is presenting demonstration number one. Students are attending closely, because they want to help the presenter to do well, and they know they will be held accountable for post-test items. Also, they realize that their turn as presenter is coming, and they want to cooperate in order to receive cooperation when they teach. The teacher spends an equal amount of time with each group listening to demonstrations. When a presenter concludes his lesson, the teacher passes out post-tests to members of his group. After the test items are checked, the teacher reads the answer key as students score the number of correct items. The total number of correct answers is tabulated for each demonstration presenter. For example, if there are ten items on the post-test, four students' composite scores could total a high of forty. So the demonstrator's score might read "thirty-one correct out of a possible score of fifty." Finally, performance checklist items are checked by students in each group, and the forms are presented to the teacher for scoring and tabulation. Later, during a personal conference period, teacher and students share information and compare notes and impressions.

CLASSROOM SCENE 2

Twenty-five students in a third-grade math class have been divided into five small teams of equal number. Operating as a team, each group must demonstrate a different concept to the other members of the class using concrete objects. A demonstration plan, given to each team one day prior to presentation, includes a math concept, a description of what students should be able to do in order to demonstrate the concept, subject matter content, operational procedures, and teaching suggestions. Working with the direction and supervision of the teacher, members of each small group have negotiated team duties and responsibilities. Group presentations will be evaluated on the basis of team performance using a checklist prepared by the teacher and distributed to students. Group presentations will also be evaluated on the basis of the number of students in class who are able to demonstrate the concept correctly using concrete objects at their desks.

On presentation day, Team One demonstrates the concept that four equal fourths of any object is one. Members of the group have an apple, a pie plate, a ball, a pencil, and a piece of cardboard, and all are divided into fourths. Different individuals put the objects together and take them apart as they name the parts: "One-fourth; two-fourths, or one-half; three-fourths; one ball."

In each case, the four equal parts become a whole object. Then team members ask each other to identify each part as they add fourths to make a whole object. To evaluate the learning objective, each student receives cardboard cutouts of different sizes, and they are asked to make one whole square within one minute. The teacher scores, tabulates, and records the total number of correct responses, and students mark the items on the group performance checklist.

The remaining four teams demonstrate similar mathematical concepts, using different ideas and approaches. Each demonstration group finishes the lesson in approximately fifteen minutes. A number of students express the opinion that the time certainly has gone by in a hurry.

Scene One depicts high school students assuming individual responsibility for teaching members of their team, while Scene Two depicts elementary school students operating as class members. The team-teaching plan allows the teacher to provide more direction and assistance during planning. Because only one lesson at a time is being presented, the teacher is able to direct attention to the lesson and the learners. The team-teaching procedure enables the teacher to influence the behavior of students and to maintain discipline, but there are ego and social problems involved, because students have to negotiate roles and duties for teaching. The teacher is able to evaluate team performance, but the evaluation of individual effort and performance is difficult. However, individual responsibility for teaching team members in a small group allows for independent responsibility. Evaluation of student's performance is an easy task for peers, but the teacher has a difficult time attempting to evaluate five or six student groups simultaneously. Confusion and discipline problems may erupt if students have not attained the maturity for working well in groups. Still, when students prepare and demonstrate a lesson independently to a small number of supporting peers, the teaching-learning experience can be very beneficial for presenter and learner.

Which of the two techniques a teacher would choose would depend on the students' experiences with group processes. The subject matter and the age and grade level of the students are inconsequential. As a prerequisite for peer teaching, students should demonstrate social and behavioral competencies. These may be taught during whole-group discussion and small-group discussion, as well as during small-group problem-solving sessions dealing with simple tasks.

Small-group peer teaching involves students as teachers and learners. Their effectiveness is evaluated by the teacher and peers, and they are held accountable as presenters and learners. The old adage that "one really learns something when one teaches it" is applicable to students involved in small-group peer teaching. Peer teaching offers students a respite from teacher-directed instruction, which sometimes causes students and teachers to become adversaries. During peer teaching, students and teacher are partners, engaged in a cooperative venture aimed at common teaching-learning outcomes.

Small-group peer teaching is not meant to replace teacher instruction. In fact, too much emphasis on small-group peer teaching has a saturation effect on students. They may begin to have doubts about the teacher's role in the instructional process. But when teachers use the method with discretion, the educational and social outcomes make it worthwhile for all concerned.

TEXTBOOK DRAMATIZATIONS

CLASSROOM SCENE 1

Twenty students in a third-grade reading class have been divided into four achievement-level groups. Students in each group are reading stories from basal texts at their particular reading level. For today's lesson, each group has been directed to act out its story with speech and movement before other members of the class.

As the members of each group read their story together, the teacher goes from group to group, helping the children to read and understand the story. The length and difficulty of each group's story is commensurate with the students' reading abilities. So groups finish their stories at about the same time.

The teacher calls "time-out" and leads the whole class in a discussion about acting out the scenes of their stories using the dialogue of the characters. They do not have to memorize parts, use costumes, or obtain scenery or props. They may improvise and pretend that these things are already there. The teacher explains that each group must decide how many parts will be included, which students will act out each part, whether groups will read the story while acting or act the story from memory, and how all members of the group may be included in the enactment.

During the planning stage, the teacher moves from group to group, making suggestions, clarifying issues, moderating differences, and answering questions. A time limit of ten minutes has been agreed upon by students, so group members are intensely involved in completing their preparation. The teacher waits until each group has completed the preparation before moving students from small-group formation into a demonstration formation for story dramatizations.

During the presentations, students create thoughts and feelings of the characters by pretending that they are actually the characters they are depicting. Observing classmates are attentive, not only because they are enjoying the dramatizations, but also because they know from past experience that they will be included in an evaluative session to find out how the dramatization might be improved.

After the dramatizations, there is a period of evaluation by the students. With the teacher serving as discussion leader, characterizations are critiqued and replayed. Scenes are discussed, and suggestions are made about better ways of presenting certain parts of the story. Finally, a list of points for improvement is compiled.

CLASSROOM SCENE 2

Groups of students have helped a high school English teacher transform the front of her classroom into a scene from *King Lear*. Students from five different classes met with the teacher on Friday to make backdrop scenery from large cardboard boxes. The scenes are not spectacular, but candles help to obliterate the distinct lines of the cardboard designs so that the room does look like the actual scene depicted in the text.

During the week preceding the dramatizations, students in each class were divided into three groups of equal numbers. Team One planned to dramatize a portion of the drama as it was written. Team Two planned to dramatize the same scenes, but they translated the language to modern standard English. Members of Team Three planned to present the same scenes using laguage used by the high school students of today.

Teams had to prepare carefully to portray the characters honestly and with the proper amount of intensity and emotion. Initially, as members of each team read the assigned scenes, they paused to discuss feelings and actions, and individual students demonstrated how certain lines should be presented. After everyone had assimilated the material, the necessary translations had been written, and students in each group had actions of characters and meanings of their speeches clearly in mind, roles were selected by members of each group.

During small-group practice sessions, students developed their characterizations by experimenting while other students appraised and evaluated the portrayals. Eventually, group members were satisfied with the preparation and felt they were ready for large-group presentation.

The teacher serves as a stimulating director of the entire project. Students have been taught to work in groups, so group work is businesslike. This allows the teacher to spend time with each group. Sometimes she offers suggestions or moderates a discussion, but most of the time students do their own thinking, and the final dramatization is their own creation.

On presentation day, each group presents its dramatization as clearly and as honestly as possible under the circumstances. Then the whole class, under the direction of the teacher, discusses and analyzes the depicted scenes. This discussion includes a period of evaluation by students so that points for improvement may be listed for future dramatizations.

Textbook dramatization may involve students in considerable preparation as it did in the high school literature class, but only minimal preparation is needed for a dramatization of most lessons in math, social studies, music, homemaking, language arts, or foreign language classes, since there is no need for script, scenery, costumes, or makeup.

Dramatizing textbook lessons adds extra dimension to the written word, and students profit from the experience in these ways:

Students comprehend the subject matter better as they dramatize it.

Students become more interested in lessons that involve them as active participants.

Dramatization helps develop the student's ability to express himself in a group situation.

Dramatizing the textbook material offers the student an alternative to reading and memorizing a text for testing purposes.

Dramatization helps students to develop their imaginations as they gain skill in the use of their actions and voice.

Dramatizing a lesson improves students' abilities in problem-solving.

Students gain a sense of responsibility because teacher and students are involved in a learning experience in which everyone is held accountable for the learning product.

Hopefully, teachers will not react negatively to this repeated warning concerning all student-centric methods: *The method must be taught to students.* Merely involving them in the method without teaching them how to operate intelligently will result in failure for teacher and student. In textbook dramatizations, the evaluation of the dramatization process and the determination of ways in which the student roles and teacher duties may be improved are integral parts of the lesson. Classroom dramatizations are a common teaching method in America, but too often the improvement of dramatization as a teaching method is left to chance. Ineffective teaching of dramatized lessons to students will result in mundane, monotonous, sterile learning experiences.

SIMULATIONS AND SIMULATING GAMES

CLASSROOM SCENE 1

Members of a fifth-grade class are studying a unit on the western states of America. A large map of the western states is draped across a section of the side wall. Students' names are pinned to the map at various points. It resembles a map a general might keep in his office for locating positions of his troops during war. The map is both political and topographical, and the tagged names are in different colors, making the large map informative and attractive. Each student has a small map that is identical to the large map. He also has a small toy car with which he is making his simulated trip. On this day, two members of the class are reporting orally about interesting scenes and sites that they have observed on their journey. One student is reporting about San Francisco, using slides that he and his family took when they visited San Francisco the preceding summer. Another student is using commercial pictures and information from an encyclopedia and from commercial literature to report on a simulated trip through Carlsbad Caverns, New Mexico. After the presentations, the oral reporters hand out a list of special points to be remembered about their reports to the other students and the teacher. During the follow-up discussion, the two students discuss the next part of their trip and then reset their name tags on the large wall map.

CLASSROOM SCENE 2

Twenty members of a secondary school homemaking class have been divided into four teams to compete for team points while playing a consumer buying game. Each student receives fifty dollars in play money with which she buys a week's supply of food for a family of four. A simulated grocery store has been set up in the classroom with the names and prices of the products marked on each container. Each student is scored on the basis of nutrition, economy, and need. Team members may plan and confer with other team members before buying, but during the actual purchasing time, each student must select her own items. Team scores are computed by counting the amount of money a team has after shopping and by adding up the nutritional values of the food chosen for the weekly meal plan. (Each food is rated on a nutritional scoring chart.)

Today, students are selecting grocery items for the week. After they have completed buying, each student passes by a checkout counter where her grocery bill is tabulated. Then she returns to a home-base planning area to plan her meals for the week.

The simulation described in Scene One is an operating

imitation of the real-life process. The game depicted in Scene Two is also an imitation of real life processes, but in Scene Two teams are formed to contest other teams for the purpose of winning. The simulation is a continuation of the method students have used to gain knowledge all their lives. When youngsters ride stick-horses, play house, or drive imaginary cars, they are learning by simulating real-life activities. They start pretending very early and continue throughout their lives. Hundreds of different games simulating athletic contests, war and peace, interpersonal relations, international relations, business transactions, and other real-life situations are bought by both children and adults. Many young people like to play games to win. During a contest-type simulation, the motive to win is a built-in incentive for complete participation. If harnessed correctly, this incentive leads to increased learning for most students.

But if teachers allow "playing the game" to supersede the attainment of learning outcomes, simulation methods of teaching will deteriorate into play, and the learning results will be minimal. To avoid this occurrence, students must be taught how to pretend and how to play simulation games so that real learning will occur. Teachers should be able to list the instructional objectives for each lesson. Immediately following the simulated situation, teacher and students can determine what they learned by interacting orally and then listing shared ideas on a flip-board. Later, this list can be duplicated, and each student can file the information in a folder for future reference and review study. The discussion session permits the teacher to examine learning outcomes in relation to instructional objectives.

Some individuals experience confusion when attempting to relate the game to the real-life situation. As a result, students play inappropriate roles, and the simulation loses its impact for students and teachers. One way to improve the simulation experience is to critique and analyze the simulated situations carefully on the basis of ways to improve role playing and game playing. This will insure that the activity is worthwhile.

Often, teachers do not supplement simulation techniques with other methods of teaching. Just as some teachers become obsessed with the lecture method, others use simulated situations to excess. A balance of methods that suits the individual teacher, the students being taught, and the particular learning situation should be maintained.

Still, simulated situation methods offer teachers many challenging opportunities to involve students in learning situations. Proponents claim that such methods have these advantages:

1. Students are actively engaged in a learning situation based on a real-life situation.
2. Simulated situations are popular with the students and are meaningful to them.
3. Simulated situations require students to use different types of thinking.
4. Students put the results of their thinking into practice and receive feedback on how effective their thinking was.
5. During simulations, the teacher is not the star of the class; he does not judge and pass sentence on student contributions. Instead, participating students are in the spotlight.
6. Simulated situations allow students to interact with, and learn from, each other.

DISCOVERY METHODS

CLASSROOM SCENE 1

Thirty members of a sixth-grade class are involved in a lesson on density. They have been divided into six social groups, with five members in each group. Each student has received a small glass vial and small containers of different colored liquids. As an introduction to the lesson, the teacher explains that each student, with help from group members, is to place the liquids into the vial in such a way that they resemble the colors of a rainbow.

After twenty minutes, most of the students have accomplished the assigned task and are eager to talk about the implications. Students contribute all the concepts and generalizations learned from the experiment, and the teacher lists them on a flip-board so that the important points can be compiled, duplicated, and distributed to students.

During the sharing stage of the lesson, the teacher carefully helps students to probe by questioning him until the desired learning outcomes are met.

CLASSROOM SCENE 2

The teacher in a tenth-grade class in social studies is teaching a lesson on "How We Think" using open inquiry. The teacher identifies the problem by relating the following anecdote:

A typical husband and wife are saying their morning goodbyes as the husband prepares to leave for his day at the office. He kisses his wife and gets into his car and leaves for work. During the ride to his office, he suddenly takes a U-turn and heads for home. As soon as he reaches the driveway, he jumps out of his car, races into the house, grabs his gun from the hall closet, and shoots his wife. Why?

The teacher explains to the students that they should solve the problem by asking him questions but that he can only answer *yes* or *no*.

After the students have reached a solution, the teacher divides the class into small special groups to discover the sequential steps which were taken in order to solve the problem.

Throughout life, students are faced with learning situations that require problem-solving. If students learn to discover answers for themselves using scientific methods, then learning through discovery will become a way of life. A citizen learning by the discovery method is more discerning than one learning by rote, because he finds solutions to problems personally instead of merely accepting the solutions of others. Teaching would be a simple profession if the only methods used were presentation methods that emphasized rote learning. But in the final analysis, learning must be initiated by the learner. Students need many opportunities to discover answers to problems, and they have to be taught how to find solutions systematically and scientifically.

Controversy exists among educators concerning structured discovery versus free, or open, discovery. Proponents of free discovery believe that when the teacher knows the answer and guides students toward appropriate solutions, then the teacher is usurping the student's right to find answers for himself. Proponents of guided discovery believe that free discovery may result in inappropriate learning outcomes, loss of important time, and placement of too much of the learning burden on the student. Teachers should try both methods and adopt a discovery method that best suits his individual teaching style, the type of student he teaches, and the particular school situation.

When teaching students how to discover solutions to

problems, the critiquing period is the critical stage of the lesson. Here, a teacher may use tape recordings to review the effectiveness of the questions asked. The students can discuss the sequential steps taken, their weaknesses and successes, ways for improvement, and their operational format on the basis of individual contributions. Records should be kept so that students may use them to gauge improvement.

In Scene Two, the lesson was conducted to teach the general steps one takes to solve problems scientifically. After students discovered the solution to the problem outlined by the teacher (the man returns to his home and shoots his wife because when the radio announcer phoned his home, a man answered), the students explored the sequential steps that were taken to find the solution. Then they compared their lists with recognized lists of steps in scientific research and steps in disciplined thought.

SUMMARY

Teachers should follow one basic rule when using student-centric methods: proceed slowly from structured situations to less structured situations. A teacher should feel competent using a whole-class discussion method before attempting small-group discussions. He should teach students successfully by using simulations before he attempts the simulated game technique. A teacher who does not interact with students in ways that establish rapport and nurture discipline may experience chaos when attempting to organize and teach using a simulated situation.

Another rule that should be repeated here is "Don't ride a good horse to death!" So often teachers do not supplement their favorite technique with the many other creative methods.

In closing, it might be useful to state that teachers operate in their classrooms on the basis of a set of beliefs that undergird everything they do. They are willing to adopt a suggested methodology if they are allowed to practice it first. If they are successful using the method and actually believe that the method is a good one for them, they will eagerly accept it as a part of their teaching repertoire. Therefore, teachers should be given the opportunity to practice the various student-centric methods, and hopefully they will adapt the methods to their respective teaching styles. Satisfactory learning results will cause students and teachers to endorse student-centric methods as being relevant to students.

SUGGESTED READINGS

BEYER, BARRY K. *Inquiry in the Social Studies Classroom.* Columbus, Ohio: Charles E. Merrill Publishing Co., 1971.

CARTWRIGHT, DORWIN, and ZANDER, ALVIN. *Group Dynamics: Research and Theory.* 3rd ed. New York: Harper & Row, 1968.

ESBENSON, THORWALD. *Working With Individualized Instruction.* Belmont, Calif.: Fearon Publishers, 1968.

GETZELS, JACOB W., and JACKSON, PHILIP W. *Creativity and Intelligence.* New York: John Wiley & Sons, 1962.

GIBBONS, MAURICE. *Individualized Instruction.* New York: Teachers College Press, Columbia University, 1971.

GOLDMARK, BERNICE. *A Method of Inquiry.* Belmont, Calif.: Wadsworth Publishing Co., 1968.

GORMAN, ALFRED H. *Teachers and Learners: the Interactive Process of Education.* 2nd ed. Boston: Allyn and Bacon, 1974.

GUETZKOW, HAROLD. *Simulation in Social Science.* Englewood Cliffs, N.J.: Prentice-Hall, 1962.

HEARN, EDELL M., and REDDICK, THOMAS. *Simulated Behavioral Teaching Situations.* Dubuque, Ia: William C. Brown Co., 1971.

HIRSCH, WERNER. *Inventing Education for the Future.* San Francisco: Chandler Publishing Co., 1967.

HOOVER, KENNETH H. *A Handbook for High School Teachers.* Boston: Allyn and Bacon, 1970.

HOOVER, KENNETH H., and HOLLINGSWORTH, PAUL M. *A Handbook for Elementary School Teachers.* Boston: Allyn and Bacon, 1973.

HYMAN, RONALD T. *Ways of Teaching.* New York: J. B. Lippincott Co., 1970.

MARDMENT, ROBERT, and BRONSTEIN, RUSSELL H. *Simulation Games: Design and Implementation.* Columbus, O.: Charles E. Merrill Publishing Co., 1973.

MATTERSON, E. M. *Play and Playthings for the Pre-School Child.* Baltimore: Penguin Books, 1973.

MORINE, HAROLD, and MORINE, GRETA. *Discovery: A Challenge to Teachers.* Englewood Cliffs, N.J.: Prentice-Hall, 1973.

POPHAM, JAMES W., and BAKER, EVAL. *Classroom Instructional Tactics.* Englewood Cliffs, N.J.: Prentice-Hall, 1973.

SHANKMAN, FLORENCE V., and KRANSYIK, ROBERT. *How to Teach Reference and Research Skills.* Englewood Cliffs, N.J.: Prentice-Hall, 1964.

STANFORD, GENE, and STANFORD, BARBARA DODDS. *Learning Discussion Skills through Games.* New York: Citation Press, 1969.

TURNBULL, WILLIAM B. *New Approaches to Individualizing Instruction.* Princeton, N.J.: Educational Testing Service, 1965.

VON HADEN, HERBERT I., and KING, JEAN MARIE. *Innovations in Education.* Worthington, O.: Charles A. Jones Publishing Co., 1971.

II. Instructional Formations for Effective Learning

How would you like to be invited to a party at someone's house and have the hostess seat you in a row formation so that you are looking at the backs of the necks of all the other guests, who are facing the hostess?

How would you like to attend concerts, films, lectures, and sports events and always have to sit in the back row, even though you paid the same price for a ticket as spectators who always sit in the front or middle rows?

Would you want the furniture in your home or office to be in the same place day in and day out for a year so that you would be forced to sit in one spot no matter what your activity, for about six hours every day?

If you had control of the seating arrangements in each of the mentioned situations, you would certainly choose the arrangement that fit the occasion best. Similarly, students in classrooms should be seated in formations that place them in the best situation for maximum learning opportunities. However, some schools in America still bolt students' desks and chairs to the floor, and others keep desks and chairs in rows where they are as stationary as they would be if they were bolted to the floor. All sorts of reasons are offered by those who want to keep a fixed seating arrangement:

> *"It is too much trouble to move furniture and students to fit activities."*

> *"I cannot control students when they move about because discipline gets out of hand."*

> *"Students have always sat in rows!"*

> *"Moving furniture causes housekeeping problems, and I don't believe moving furniture causes students to learn more."*

But most of these reasons are usually rationalizations used by people resistant to change.

If all students learned in precisely the same manner or reacted to classroom situations in the same way, then teachers could place all students in rows and mass teach them by using the same methods over and over again. Although many teachers do practice this type of teaching methodology, evidence clearly points to the fact that students have different learning styles. Therefore, teachers should use a variety of instructional formations so that each student may experience, at least a part of the time, a learning situation that best suits his particular learning style.

Even if educational gain did not result from particular instructional formations, it should be evident to everyone that students need to see each other face to face when they discuss topics with each other. During presentations and demonstrations, each student should be seated in the best position for observing the performance, and certainly, students should move from place to place during the school day.

These general considerations should be weighed before any particular formation is put into operation:

1. A home-base formation should provide teacher and students with a number of optional teaching-learning situations so that students may spend a considerable portion of their day at their home base rather than shifting continually from one special formation to another.
2. Some formations are more useful for teacher-centric methods of teaching, while other formations accommodate student-centric methods. The formation chosen for each lesson should suit the teaching method being used and provide a teaching-learning environment that is the very best for all concerned.
3. Many practices in the public schools are based on tradition. To implement change is difficult and, in some cases, unrewarding, but a change toward increased effectiveness is worth the price. Community and administrative support are necessary; however, involvement and successful experiences with the proposed change should be considered before implementation procedures.
4. Which formations to use depends on these factors: space, people, desired climate, the type of room, and equipment (including desks, chairs, tables, and other furniture).

Choosing the appropriate instructional formation allows teachers to focus on the learner, which results in more effective learning. The purpose here is to present a variety of instructional formations, to offer suggestions for making them flexible, and to suggest ways to encourage teachers to use them.

HOME-BASE FORMATIONS

Regardless of which administrative plan a school system or school building uses to organize students into learning groups, all students need a basic instructional formation. A home-base formation allows each student to have a space area, including furniture, that gives him a feeling of permanency and security. But while a home-base formation should stay in effect long enough to provide students with feelings of stability and security, the formation should be changed often enough to provide for variety and differences in tastes of students and teachers.

There are a number of home-base formations that teachers find beneficial for students and teaching situations. Following are diagrams, descriptions, and uses of some of the most popular.

Vertical Rows (Figure 2.1)

Probably the most popular formation for classroom instruction is the traditional vertical-rows formation. Because students have sat in this formation since the beginning of public education in America, some teachers feel secure operating from this type of formation. Many parents feel that their children are really learning when they look through the classroom doorway and observe students working diligently

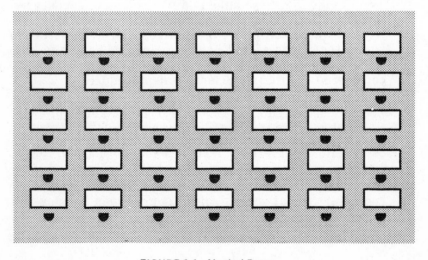

FIGURE 2.1   Vertical Rows

and quietly at desks placed in rows, just as they were when the parents went to school.

At times, vertical rows may be the best home-base formation to use, but teachers need to be aware of its limitations as a full-time formation. Following is a list of the advantages and limitations of vertical rows as a home-base formation.

ADVANTAGES

Useful for independent seatwork
Facilitates housekeeping
Useful for presentations
Useful for recitations
Facilitates monitoring chores
Allows use of row-completion games
Helps the teacher control students
Encourages children to listen
Convenient for giving tests

LIMITATIONS

Gives children unequal seating status
Prevents interaction among students
Gives all students the same instructional package
May result in poor eye contact with some students in the back of the room
Teacher is the star

Horizontal Rows (Figure 2.2)

Horizontal rows proved teachers with a structured home-base formation that places students closer to the scene of the

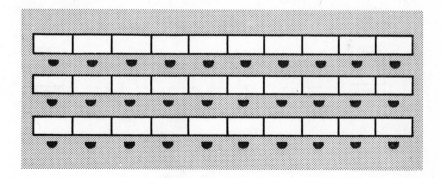

FIGURE 2.2   Horizontal Rows

action. In this formation, they are in a position to interact to a small degree with a peer both socially and academically. The uses and limitations are similar to those of vertical-row formations with some major differences.

ADVANTAGES

Useful for independent seatwork
Encourages children to listen
Permits children to work in pairs
Allows a walking teacher to check seatwork easily
Facilitates housekeeping
Useful for presentations
Useful for recitations
Useful for demonstrations
Facilitates monitoring

LIMITATIONS

Results in poor interaction among students
Teacher is the star
Students spend most of their time listening, writing, and reading
All students receive the same instructional package

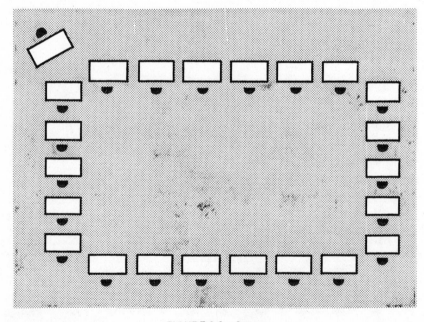

FIGURE 2.3   Square

Square (Figure 2.3)

Teachers who like to deviate from traditional rows for a home base formation while still maintaining structure for discipline purposes may choose the square. The square allows equal seating status for students while still maintaining many of the uses attributed to rows.

ADVANTAGES

Permits independent study
Permits interaction among students
Useful for discussion
Useful for symposiums
Allows children more space in which to move about
Center area good for center stage
Useful for demonstrations
Home-base formation

LIMITATIONS

Poor for whole-group presentations
Poor for films and other audience situations
Could cause special problems for school custodian
Affects teacher's ability to control the children

Circle (Figure 2.4)

The circle as a home-base formation is very similar to the square. The same uses and use limitations apply to both formations.

Cross or Wheel (Figure 2.5)

The cross, or wheel, formation is a good arrangement when areas of the room are needed for special displays, interest centers, interest stations, or activity areas. But children should not be kept in this formation for an extended period of time.

ADVANTAGES

Permits independent study
Useful for open-space activities
Allows room for interest areas

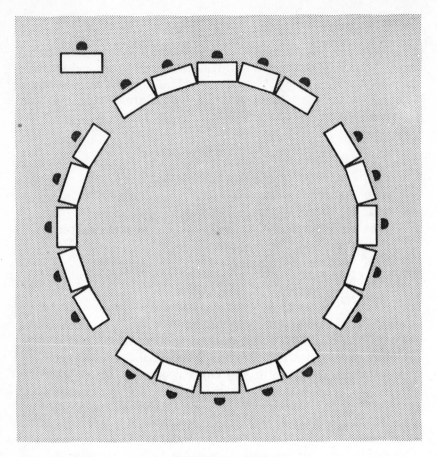

FIGURE 2.4   Circle

Allows room for interest centers
Allows teacher to teach students who are studying differ-
    ent subjects, units, topics, or lessons
Convenient for giving tests

LIMITATIONS

Poor for presentations, films, or listening
Not for interaction lessons at desks
Poor for whole-group activity

Facing Groups of Four (Figure 2.6)

The facing-groups-of-four formation offers many opportunities for students to interact. They learn how to operate

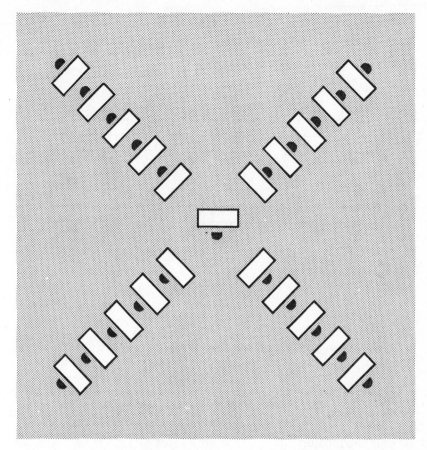

FIGURE 2.5 Cross or Wheel

individually and as members of a small group. This formation is a basic formation for many student-centric teaching methods. However, since this is not a tightly structured formation, it should not be used by teachers who have not established disciplinary boundaries and procedures with students.

ADVANTAGES
Encourages student interaction
Allows sharing of equipment and supplies
Useful for all types of group work
Useful for student-centric teaching methods

LIMITATIONS
Poor for lectures
Poor for presentations

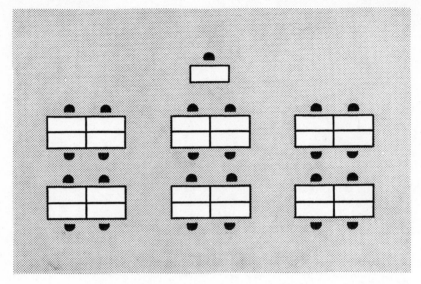

FIGURE 2.6   Facing Groups of Four

Poor for any whole-class teaching
Cliques may form if the formation is used for a long period

Pairs (Figure 2.7)

A pair formation offers a wide variety of uses, as well as limitations. Placing students in pairs is an introductory step toward placing them in larger groups, because many of the social skills for getting along with one person are necessary for getting along with a larger number of students. All types of groups, such as achievement level, needed skills, social, polar, and interest, may be formed by two class members in preparation for the same types of groups with a greater number of participants.

ADVANTAGES

Useful for all presentation methods
Useful for all types of group methods
Useful for seatwork—Special projects
Useful for all types of individual and group activities
Allows teacher to use both teacher-centric and student-
    centric methods

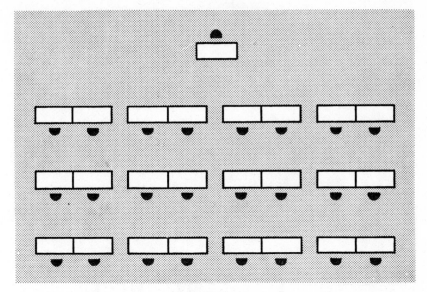

FIGURE 2.7 Pairs

LIMITATIONS

Pairs are static

Partners may be unhappy together

Pair members could become too dependent on each other

Pair members may not be compatible (one worker, one learner—cannot resolve differences)

May stifle individuality as pair members adapt to a paired situation

U Formation (Figure 2.8)

The U formation is actually three sides of a square, but the open space at the front permits more flexibility and diversification. Presentations, films, lectures, and recitations may be conducted, as well as discussions and group work.

ADVANTAGES

Useful for independent seatwork

Useful for group work

Useful for discussions

Useful for panels and symposiums

Useful for structured study

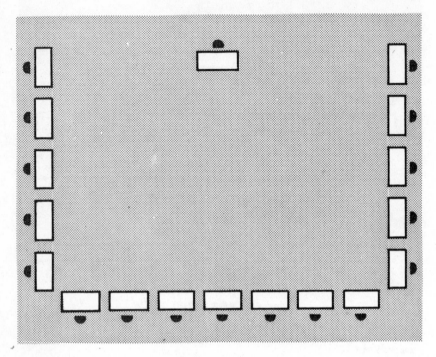

FIGURE 2.8   U Formation

Useful for lectures, presentations, recitations, and demon-
strations
Useful for film and television viewing
Provides equal seating arrangement
Has open space for center activities

LIMITATIONS

Poor for whole-class teaching
Students are not in a good position for teacher's presenta-
tion
Students are relatively removed from presentation

I Formation (Figure 2.9)

The I formation places two distinct groups of students into
one area. If the teacher wants to separate children according
to grade level, subject concentration, or achievement differences, then the I formation forms a natural barrier between
the two groups of students, allowing the teacher to operate
with each group independently.

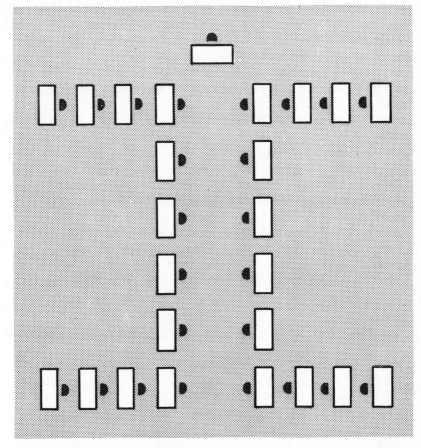

FIGURE 2.9   I Formation

ADVANTAGES

   Permits individual seatwork in two distinct groups
   Useful for classes in a multi-graded summer school
   Appropriate for all types of teaching methods

LIMITATIONS

   Divides class members
   Formation cannot be used for all purposes

SPECIAL FORMATIONS

Students at all levels of their public school life enjoy, and
profit from, moving into various special instructional forma-

tions during the school day. If the lessons are enhanced by instructional formations that accommodate what is being taught, then the few seconds that are spent changing formations is well worth the time and the effort.

Some teachers like to teach and label all the formations planned for specific learning activities at the beginning of the school term, while others prefer to teach and label each special formation as it becomes necessary just prior to the appropriate activity. It is usually necessary to have a time limit for moving from one formation to another. Noise level and behavior expectations must be taught and reinforced. Good performance should be rewarded with extrinsic and intrinsic rewards. Keep the purpose of the formation in mind at all times. If the home-base formation will achieve the same purpose, don't form a new special structure.

Following are some of the special instructional formations.

Stack Formation (Figure 2.10)

The stack formation places students and teacher closer to each other and nearer the scene of action. The formation creates a feeling of unity and "we-ness," making students feel closer emotionally. This formation should not be used often, and it should be of short duration. Once it has fulfilled the purpose for which it was formed, the formation should be broken up. This formation is especially helpful when a teacher needs complete attention from students. Eye contact and attention from students help teacher and students to concentrate on the immediate topic. Because this formation brings students close together, disciplinary procedures and expectations must be taught.

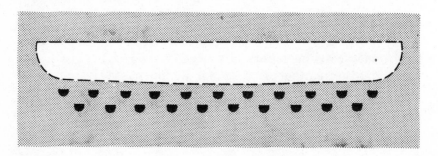

FIGURE 2.10   Stack Formations

ADVANTAGES

Useful for presentations
Useful for demonstrations
Facilitates teacher-student planning
Useful for chalkboard sharing, flannel-board sharing, and flip-board sharing
Convenient storytelling
Useful for brainstorming
Useful for panels and symposiums
Useful for sociodramas
Useful for filmstrips
Useful for informal lectures
Useful for mediated lectures
Useful for media presentations
Useful for evaluative sessions

Whole-Group Formation (Figure 2.11)

The whole-group formation is the only way to arrange thirty or forty students into a discussion situation where everyone is involved, and it is the only formation in which true discussion may be taught.

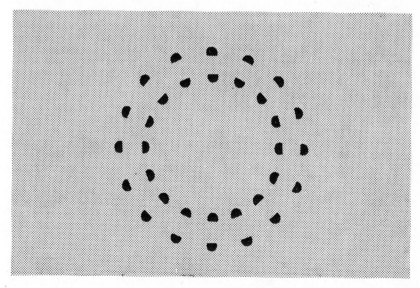

FIGURE 2.11   Whole-Class Discussion

This formation places the emphasis for learning on student participation. Students learn by involvement. Their experiences are not aimless, since constant evaluations of discussion techniques are made by participants, peers, and teacher.

Round-Table Discussion (Figure 2.12)

The round-table discussion formation places eight participants, who have prepared well in advance, around a table. Round-table participants have a dual responsibility—to present and to discuss. The other class members surround the participants in a formation that allows everyone to see and to listen to the round-table participants. After the round-table members present and discuss for fifteen or twenty minutes, everyone joins in the discussion, asking questions, making comments, or debating points. The round-table formation involves the whole class in the activity in a meaningful manner after the initial presentation by round-table discussion members.

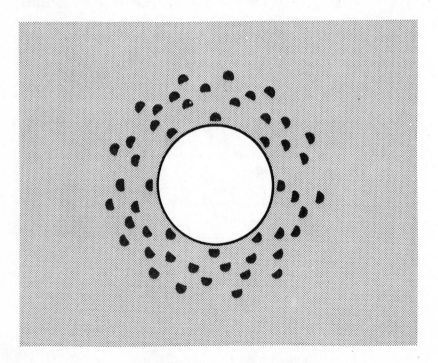

FIGURE 2.12   Round-Table Discussion

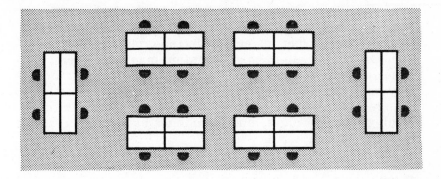

FIGURE 2.13   Small-Group Discussion

Small-Group Discussion (Figure 2.13)

If facing-groups-of-four is the home-base formation, changing into a small-group formation for buzz groups, committee work, work sessions, or discovery lessons might be a waste of time. When using any of the other home-base formations,

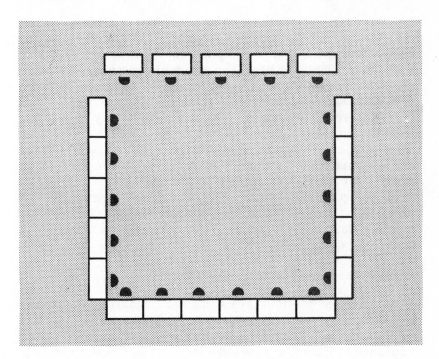

FIGURE 2.14   Individual Work Formation

however, it is good practice to change to a small-group formation when information is to be shared. Sometimes this change
is useful even when using the facing-groups-of-four formation, for each group in that formation may have been determined to achieve a specific purpose, and teacher and students
may prefer to move into a special small-group formation to
change group membership to achieve a different purpose.
Small-group procedures and techniques have been discussed
in detail in Chapter 1.

Individual-Work Formation (Figure 2.14)

The individual-work formation is a special formation designed
to allow students to concentrate on an important independent
task. This formation is especially adaptable for taking standardized tests or for completing programmed modules. It is
also a good arrangement for machine and computer stations.
Since this formation is designed for one purpose, it should be
dissolved as soon as that purpose has been achieved.

Interest Stations (Figure 2.15)

Interest stations are primarily instructional centers designed
to teach a concept or a related group of concepts in a variety
of ways. The stations may be designed to teach different
concepts that lead to overall goals and objectives.

Interest stations may be used effectively in a team-
teaching situation. Each member of the team is the instructional leader of an interest station, and at a designated time
either teachers or students move in a carrousel rotation
pattern from one interest station to the next.

Instructional leaders may also teach a group of children the same concept at each interest station, then conduct
a whole-class sharing session after the station lesson.

Interest Centers (Figure 2.16)

While interest stations are designed primarily for instructional purposes and are dissolved after one lesson or one day,
interest centers are placed in the classroom to accommodate
and enrich students' interests in certain areas on a long-
range basis.

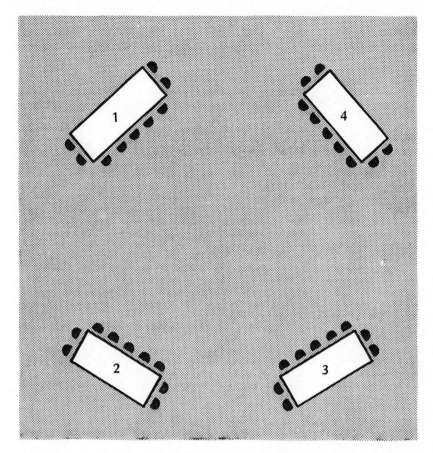

FIGURE 2.15 Interest Stations

Successful centers are designed well so that students anticipate spending time in the area to pursue the ideas presented there. Too many centers are designed and built on the basis of teacher interest and expertise instead of student interest and involvement. After a period of time, depending on the popularity and effectiveness of the center, the center should be dissolved and another center should be built to accommodate other interests.

Interest centers may be built around any interest. Some of the most common centers include recreational reading centers, creative writing centers, listening to music centers, science centers, mathematics problems and games centers, project centers, and special centers for departmentalized subjects.

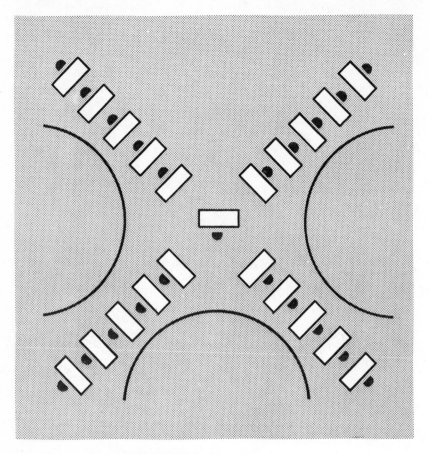

FIGURE 2.16   Interest Centers

Whole-Class Debate (Figure 2.17)

The whole-class-debate formation is designed to separate students on opposing teams so that students on one side of the issue will be facing students arguing the opposing view. The space separating the two teams also serves as a space station for the teacher-moderator. This is the best formation for whole-class debate, but it has very little to offer for other activities, so the formation is a short-term one and should be dissolved as soon as the activity is terminated.

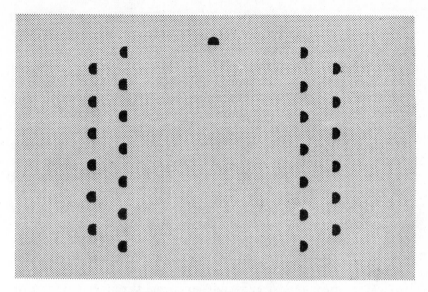

FIGURE 2.17   Whole-Class Debate Formation

INTRODUCING INSTRUCTIONAL FORMATIONS
TO THE TEACHER

Teachers operate in a teaching-learning situation according
to a set of attitudes and beliefs about themselves that has a
direct relationship to how they feel about others. Regardless
of administrative policies or community pressures, teachers
do not violate their basic beliefs. Their roles during the school
day are based on their philosophy of life and philosophy of
education.

Teachers are willing to change practices only if the
proposed change is congruent with their fundamental
ideologies—and then, only if the proposed change works for
them, resulting in a better teaching-learning situation as
they see it.

The organizational format for implementing a variety
of instructional formations should be much more extensive
than mere administrative edict or faculty meetings designed
to explain why and how to teach using multiple formations.
Sessions should be designed to allow teachers to experience

each instructional formation from a learner's point of view. Such sessions would allow teachers to learn the methodology while at the same time determining how they feel about it. Concurrently, the different formations should be modeled with the teacher in her teaching location. Then, teachers and students should be videotaped as they experience the student-centric teaching methods that occur because of the instructional formation. As teachers meet with videotape feedback consultants, they learn to critique and to evaluate their own lessons in light of program objectives. Special aid and encouragement can be provided for those teachers asking for additional help.

Of course, a program of this sort can be effective only if the administrative personnel, especially the building principals, believe that multiple formations are actually worthwhile. Administrators can be very influential by supporting and implementing multiple formations on a continuing basis.

The increase in creative learning through student involvement and interaction will provide reason enough for the teacher to use and adapt instructional formations continually to meet students' needs.

III. Specific Suggestions for Intra-Classroom Grouping Procedures

Achievement-Level Groups

Needed-Skills Groups

Implementing Achievement-Level Groups and Needed-Skills Groups in a Spelling Program

Interest Groups

Social Groups

Special-Purpose Groups

Implementing Interest Groups, Social Groups, and Special-Purpose Groups in an American History Class

Suggestions for Effective Grouping

During the early years of education in the United States, students attended a one-room school where one teacher taught all students, regardless of their age or educational achievement level. In some situations, all the students were taught in one large group. At other times, groups of students were taught in subgroup formations on the basis of achievement levels. Other teaching-learning situations included students teaching and helping other students in groups designed for this purpose; groups of all ages working together on topics and projects in which they were interested; students arranged in pairs; and students learning alone on individual assignments and projects. Teachers of one-room schools were forced to group students within the classroom in order to meet their diverse educational needs. Not only did they have to teach every subject to students ranging in age from six to eighteen, but they also had to accommodate instructional levels to the students' abilities, organizing different lessons for a number of groups and individuals.

The industrial revolution resulted in an enormous increase in student population, which led school systems to organize students into class groups based on chronological age. When students of the same age were placed together in graded schools, a pernicious myth spread throughout the country: Students of the same age are alike and can be expected to learn at the same rate; therefore, teachers can select a prescribed curriculum and teach all students at the same time and in the same way. As a result of this myth, the mass-teaching movement was instigated and became the prevalent mode of operation for a majority of the public school systems in the United States.

The mass-teaching movement, which is still in operation to a large extent, has many shortcomings. Some of the most relevant inadequacies now evident include mass educational methods that do not fit the needs of students in today's world. A great communication chasm exists between teachers and students and among students, because mass-teaching methods place a heavy emphasis on listening and writing. Students feel a personalization loss—they feel like numbers on a computer instead of feeling like breathing, living, vital human beings. Mass instructional methods relegate the teacher's role to that of being a presenter. Subject matter is structured for the average student, while the fast learner is neglected and the slow learner is eliminated.

Certainly, the one-room school is not the answer to the instructional problems that educators face in today's world, but the intra-classroom grouping procedures that allowed those teachers to meet diversified student needs can be adapted to allow today's teachers to focus on the individual learner more adequately.

For years, teachers have talked and written about intra-classroom grouping procedures, but being able to talk and to write about educational methodology is not good enough. Teaching is a performing profession, and until colleges of education incorporate performing in the public schools as an integral part of the total teacher-education programs, teachers will tend to talk and to write one game with college professors and to play an entirely different game in classrooms.

For years, school systems have grouped students for administrative and instructional purposes. The criteria and measuring schemes for grouping students into teachable units have been numerous, but regardless of which administrative grouping plan is in operation, intra-class grouping is still necessary. Merely grouping students administratively according to achievement levels in subject matter offers very little assurance that students in these groups will be alike in their social, emotional, physical, and intellectual competencies and needs, or even in their abilities to master the subject matter for which they were grouped! Administrators have attempted to solve the problem of teaching a large group of students who are different in all aspects of growth and development by placing students with similar capabilities and characteristics into classes together. But this procedure tends to confuse teachers who have been using individualized instructional practices in their classrooms, because when students are grouped administratively on the basis of likeness, teachers believe these specially grouped students are enough alike so that they can forget individualized instructional methods, and as a result they practice mass-teaching methods.

Teachers need an in-service program that helps them to implement intra-classroom grouping procedures with students in their regular classrooms. Practical suggestions for implementing intra-classroom grouping procedures will be described later in this chapter, and continuing education programs are described in Chapter 7.

ACHIEVEMENT-LEVEL GROUPS

Grouping on the basis of achievement levels is the most prevalent type of intra-classroom grouping, especially in the area of reading. In other subject matter areas, there have been isolated programs where teachers have practiced achievement grouping within the classroom. Across a broad spectrum of America, however, achievement-level grouping within the classroom is not a common practice.

By grouping on the basis of achievement, teachers do not have to teach extremely accelerated students and low-achieving students in the same group; therefore, great differences in ability to perform at a prescribed achievement level are minimized. But if assessment procedures are not administered often, and group members are not regrouped accordingly, a wide range of variance will occur within the group.

Intra-classroom achievement-level grouping is a valuable grouping procedure because it induces teachers to use formal and informal assessing instruments for measuring student achievement. As small groups of students with like abilities are formed, teachers are able to present content in relation to the students' abilities to perform. These groupings influence teachers to concentrate on student learning at different levels rather than expecting all students to attain all the content prescribed for a certain subject or grade level.

Teachers who use achievement-level grouping often think that achievement is the only basis for intra-classroom grouping. But always grouping students on the basis of achievement would be a deleterious practice, because it has certain limitations that should be ameliorated by using other types of intra-classroom grouping procedures. Dependence on achievement grouping at the expense of other types of grouping may result in a stigma's being attached to students in the low group or preferential treatment being given to students placed in the high group.

NEEDED-SKILLS GROUPS

The purpose of grouping on the basis of achievement levels is to teach members of a small group material that they can master as a group. However, a teacher who wishes to suit work to individual levels of talent still needs to regroup students on the basis of needed skills. Merely because all students in a small group have been measured as being approximately at the same achievement level in a subject, they do not necessarily need the same instruction. For example, individual students from all achievement levels may need certain map study skills in social studies; individual students in reading, regardless of their achievement level, may need to develop certain phonics skills; and certain individuals may need to develop the skill of reading for facts. There are numerous skills for students to master in all subjects, and the achievement level a particular student is supposed to have reached according to scores he has made on imperfect measuring instruments is not synonymous with the skills he has mastered—or even with what he has learned.

Using both formal and informal diagnostic instruments, individual student's needs can be determined and small groups can be formed from any whole-class group. Needed-skills grouping complements achievement-level grouping because membership in each group is different; consequently, the stigma of one's being in a low achievement-level group is decreased. And because the needed-skills grouping process focuses on individual needs while the achievement-level grouping focuses on curriculum requirements, using both groupings results in a more balanced approach to learning for all students.

One way to organize students into needed-skills groups and achievement-level groups so that both types can operate concurrently is to organize and teach each type of group on different days. If a teacher teaches more than one subject, he may organize students differently according to the subject.

Achievement-level groups and needed-skills groups can operate simultaneously. First, determine each student's achievement level and form achievement-level groups. After students have mastered the required achievement tasks while functioning as a group, then students' needed skills are diagnosed and a needed-skills group can be formed from among class members who may or may not be from the same achievement-level group. As soon as the members of the needed-skills group have mastered the skills for which the group was formed, they may return to their achievement-level group. Students should not be held responsible for learning that took place in the achievement groups while they were participating in the needed-skills group.

IMPLEMENTING ACHIEVEMENT-LEVEL GROUPS AND NEEDED-SKILLS GROUPS IN A SPELLING PROGRAM

Introduction

The accusation is made quite often by people from all walks of life that we are a nation of poor spellers. All one has to do is to observe written work in business, industry, the professions, or correspondence to realize that the "poor speller" accusation has some validity.

There are many reasons why we are a nation of poor spellers, but one of the paramount reasons is that spelling is probably the most poorly taught subject in our public schools.

If one observed a spelling lesson in a classroom in the United States each day for a week, one would more than likely see the following: On Monday, the teacher introduces the words from the basal spelling text, either by testing to see which words individual students spelled incorrectly so that they could study those words or by assigning all the students a list of words to study for the week. On Tuesday, students complete exercises from the textbook or in a workbook that supplements the textbook. On Wednesday, more exercises are completed by all students working from the same materials. On Thursday, all students review the words for the week, and on Friday, students are tested on the words for the week, and a percentage grade is placed in the grade book. An average of these grades forms the basis for reporting to parents about how well their child can spell.

Although research and experience have demonstrated that memorizing word lists does not result in one's being able to spell words needed when writing, having children memorize word lists is still the predominant method for teaching spelling. The primary reason that we are a nation of poor spellers, then, is that the public schools emphasize the teaching of word lists rather than teaching students how to spell.

Program Description

Initial steps for implementing an individualized spelling program are diagnostic steps so that teachers can find students' spelling levels and diagnose difficulties. Probably the most convenient method for finding achievement levels is to pretest students by using graded basal texts or standardized spelling tests. While the teacher is determining achievement levels, students are kept in a whole-class group, which helps the teacher to maintain discipline and establish class cohesiveness. Intra-classroom grouping will be accomplished gradually, because the social processes of grouping must be taught as diligently as the achievement task, which in this case is spelling.

A pretesting procedure will reveal that students' abilities to spell vary considerably. For example, in a third-grade class there will likely be students who are able to spell words three grades above grade level while others will only be able to spell words three grades below grade level. Even those students who are measured as being capable of spelling words on grade level are not necessarily at the same level as far as being able to spell words they need when they write.

On the basis of this pretesting program, membership for the achievement-level groups can be determined and the first group, which will be called a team, will be separated from the whole-class group. This first team may be composed of poor, average, or excellent spellers, depending on the goals and strategies of the teacher; however, this group must be taught to be a model operation that completes the prescribed task by carrying on the social processes that allow students to achieve objectives as a group.

As soon as the teacher separates the first team from the other members of the class, he will have two groups to instruct. So the whole-class group should plan together for both groups at the beginning of the period, before the two groups are separated. The planning and instructional goals for the day should be achievement-task oriented and social-behavior oriented. This planning session is extremely valuable because it prevents students from wasting time and being confused when they are separated into groups. Even more important is the whole-class evaluation session at the end of the period, when all class members are involved in the evaluation of both achievement and social objectives of the small groups.

The teacher's role for conducting the two groups simultaneously can be as diversified as his teaching plan. On different days, the teacher might conduct individual seat work with the regular class group while Team One completes a dictionary of word prefixes; Team One might take and correct a weekly post-test while the teacher teaches dictionary skills to the other class members; and both groups might complete individual seat work while the teacher conducts individual conferences concerning spelling. The teacher's role can be as diversified and creative as the individual teacher.

When two groups are operating successfully, then the third team can be disengaged from the regular class group, thus forming three achievement-level groups. Now, the teacher's role becomes more complex. Planning and conducting three teams induces teachers to use student-centric teaching methods. Consequently, students become involved to a greater extent, and lessons are planned on the students' achievement level, allowing them to accomplish tasks and experience success. The teacher's methods for grouping remain the same, but each day social processes within the group must be taught as diligently as spelling.

When teachers teach spelling to the whole group, they tend to aim the content toward the average student. So what happens when they group students on the basis of achievement? Then, teachers tend to spend more time with the low and high teams and neglect the grade-level team. But sufficient planning for each group is a prerequisite for the success of grouping. Providing for whole-group planning and instruction time at the beginning of the class period and assessment and evaluation time at the close of each period eliminates many of the problems that teachers encounter when they group students within the classroom.

One period a week should be provided for whole-group activities and games. Worthwhile activities that apply to all students include proofreading procedures, memory techniques and devices, dictionary techniques and drills, individualized spelling programs, testing and diagnosis, and all types of spelling games. One spelling game axiom is that all competitive games should be fair for *all* the game participants.

Once students have learned to reach objectives in a whole group, in a small team, and as an individual, the teacher should determine their individual needs. He should assess every need pertaining to a phase of human growth and development, including the physical, emotional, social and cognitive domains.

In the physical realm, examinations should be conducted to discover physical disabilities that might cause the student to have difficulty learning to spell. Especially important are seeing, hearing, and speaking difficulties, but other physical problems that contribute to poor spelling and other academic problems can also be diagnosed. In some cases, the physical difficulties can be remediated, but even if the problem is beyond remediation, classroom formations and teaching strategies can help students to compensate for their physical disability.

Emotional needs may be numerous and complex. A teacher's expertise in the area of psychology and psychiatry may be limited, but there are certain needs in the emotional realm that are common to all students. Everyone needs to feel liked, wanted, worthy, capable, able, trustworthy, and special as a human being, and every individual needs to have realistic goals to reach in order to experience success more often than he experiences failure. Teachers who accept themselves to the extent that they can accept students unconditionally are capable of helping students who have formed a self-concept of being inferior academically, especially those who believe they are poor spellers. When more serious emotional problems are encountered and psychological aid is not attainable, the ability to accept the student as being worthwhile, while not attempting to fit him into a preconceived mold, is more worthwhile than pseudo-psychological procedures that may do more harm than good.

To be accepted and liked by one's peers are tremendous needs that can cause students to become behavior problems when they do not receive sufficient recognition from their classmates. How students' needs in the social realm can be diagnosed and how remedial procedures can be administered will be discussed thoroughly later in this chapter.

Delving into students' needs in all facets of human growth and development allows teachers to comprehend the significance of measuring and instructing the whole child, but a fact to remember is that the primary purpose in this program is to teach students to spell. Therefore, most of the needed-skills groups will be formed from information gleaned from measuring in the cognitive domain.

General information that can provide an overview of cognitive performance in spelling can usually be found in the student's personal folder. Personal folders may be examined for IQ scores, achievement test scores, teachers' grades, health charts, and individual progress charts. All evidence found in personal folders should be kept in the proper perspective; that is, this information is only as valid and reliable as the measuring instruments used and the people who administered the tests and recorded the data. So the information is indicative, not positive; it supplies a general reference point from which a teacher may begin.

Because most individual needs in spelling are conceptual or phonetic, vocabulary and phonics tests should be administered to determine the individual needs in these critical cognitive areas.

After careful diagnosis has been made through testing and through teacher observation during spelling lessons in whole-group and achievement-level-group formation, needed-skills groups may be formed, and achievement-level groups and needed-skills groups may be rotated every other day. A needed-skills group and achievement-level groups can also operate concurrently. To illustrate: Diagnosis reveals that two students on achievement-level Team Three, two students on Team Two, and one student on Team One all miss words in context because of carelessness. After a whole-group planning session at the beginning of the period has determined goals, procedures, products, evaluation procedures, and group and individual duties and responsibilities, and after achievement-level groups are operating successfully, then a needed-skills group can be formed to teach the students to be careful. The teacher can teach proofreading skills by presenting material that the students have written and letting them underline the words misspelled. Then, when the teacher asks that these students proofread their papers for spelling errors, they will know how. As soon as the need for this group has ended, the group is disbanded and members return to their achievement-level group. Of course, instructions during the planning session should explain procedures to all class members and the needed-skills group should not be held responsible for the achievement-level group's product for the day.

A comprehensive spelling program will provide opportunities for students to learn independently. Instructional packets and independent study modules, described in Chapter 4 of this book, can be prepared for this purpose. Although teachers cannot be expected to develop programs and teach students at the same time, school systems must provide financial support for teachers to develop such materials.

One simple method for providing students with opportunities to learn to spell words they need when writing is the individualized word list method using the tape recorder as a teaching machine. With the help and encouragement of the teacher, students keep a list of the misspelled words they discover as they proofread their papers. These words may be from subject areas or personal writing (letters, diaries, notes). The word lists may also include new vocabulary words that the children would like to use in writing. The number of words per week will vary from student to student, according to the discretion of the teacher and student. One student may have a list of ten words, another may choose twenty or more.

During designated times on Mondays and Tuesdays, each student uses the tape recorder as a teaching machine. The students state their names and place numbers on the recorder, then read their words from their prepared lists. They say a word, wait long enough for the word to be written, spell the word correctly so that the correct spelling is recorded, then say the next word. During the designated time on Thursdays and Fridays, students may test themselves with the recorder, then evaluate the results. These results may be shared with the teacher and at times with a team member or members, depending on the individual student's desires and needs. Students and teacher keep a record of words learned for the year, and special emphasis is placed on the correct spelling of these words in all writing activities.

Although this is a description of a spelling program, the methodology is generic, and the strategies and techniques can be used for other subjects and at every grade level. Strategies and techniques that focus on the learner are as essential to a mathematics instructor in high school as they are to an instructor of a group of third-grade students learning to spell. Achievement-level grouping and needed-skills grouping are procedures that help teachers to focus on student learning; however, other bases for grouping should be used to augment these grouping procedures.

INTEREST GROUPS

Students of all ages have a variety of academic interests, not only in different subjects, but also within the framework of the various subjects. When students are involved with an interesting and exciting learning task, they are more willing to attempt and complete it; therefore, more real learning takes place.

Grouping on the basis of interest allows students to research topics from a variety of sources, to report findings to small and large groups orally or in writing, and to organize and develop individual and group projects as they learn to cooperate with other students in a team operation. Interest grouping offers a change from achievement-level grouping and allows the students to choose the group they want to join without any pretesting or teacher manipulation. Thus the stigma of being placed in a low group or the deleterious effect that may occur from being placed in an average or high group is nullified. Grouping on the basis of student interest is democracy in action, because the teacher and students are cooperating, planning, implementing, and evaluating together to accomplish individual and curriculum goals and objectives.

The roles of teacher and students change dramatically when a class switches from a situation where the teacher is a presenter-competitor-tester and students are listeners, note-takers, and test-takers to one where the teacher is leader-catalyst-motivator and students are participators, producers, and evaluators.

Interest groups may be formed on the basis of interest in a particular topic, interest in a task concerning the topic, or interest in both the topic and the relevant task. When a class group is learning about Mexico, for example, interest groups may be formed around such topics as tourists' spas, various cities, illicit drug farming and smuggling, industries, recreation, and Mexican peasants. Of course, this is a partial list, and the topics on Mexico could be as diverse as the students themselves. Groups may also be formed on the basis of interest in tasks, with students selecting the tasks that interest them. A partial list of tasks includes doing research and making reports, making real object displays and giving reports, preparing art and bulletin board displays and group reports, preparing media presentations, and preparing special projects and giving reports. Making the interest group topical or task-oriented is not as important initially as allowing students to choose the group they are interested in.

A rather unique way to organize students into interest groups uses interest stations. Three or four interest stations may be set up around the room for the purpose of teaching the same concept or skill, but each station employs a different strategy for teaching and learning, and the student selects the station in which he is most interested.

Say that the skill to be taught is to find the main ideas of paragraphs in a particular story. One station would include an overhead projector and screen. A student operator would show transparencies of the story, and students in groups would identify and record the main ideas of the paragraphs. Then the students would defend their choices to other students in their group.

Another station might include a tape recorder and earphones. Students would listen to paragraphs and write down the main ideas. Then they could check their individual answers against a mimeographed answer key.

A third group may be working with the teacher. He asks multiple-choice questions concerning the main ideas from a book, then the students pick the right choice and defend it.

As a follow-up activity for evaluation, the whole class could play a main-idea game. The object of the game is to select the correct main idea from a list of suggestions in order to learn a secret message. Each suggestion has a code number that supplies a message, but only the correct suggestions have code numbers that will supply part of the secret message. As students find the secret message, they write down clues to help others; thus, students are allowed to help other students.

Interest stations can also be used to teach different concepts or skills. At the close of the class period, each group can share with the rest of the class the information it learned at its interest station, or students may rotate from one station to the next.

Because interest stations are formed to teach subject-matter concepts and skills, the stations are subject-matter oriented, and the selections that students make are really choices of how they choose to learn. Student interests should definitely be kept in mind when stations are being built and materials are being chosen. Interest stations usually exist for only a day or two because the reason for their existence will expire, although the technique may be used again at another time.

Interest centers are semi-permanent areas that are stocked with material covering a specific topic or subject. Interest centers are topical or subject-matter oriented. For example, a teacher might set up a creative-writing center or a math-activity center. Students are allowed to spend time in interest centers, developing projects or merely engaging in the activities that the center provides. An interest center should be in operation only as long as it offers a real learning experience for enough students to justify its existence. Interest-center participation should be as important to the teacher and students as anything else they do during the school day.

Interest groups, interest stations, and interest centers offer teacher and students a respite from lectures, recitation, and assigned seat work study. Of course, because students have different learning styles, a variety of techniques and methods are necessary to enable teachers to reach more students, but every method must be based on sound principles of learning. During interest-group participation, the students are engaged in an active process. What they learn is meaningful, useful and interesting to them, and the focus is on the individual.

Teacher-student planning, learning by the discovery method, and evaluations based on performance and product are integral components of interest-group methodology. During the planning sessions, when goals and objectives are formulated and evaluative instruments and techniques are discussed and adopted, everyone involved should understand that interest-group activities and products must lead toward fulfillment of what is to be learned.

SOCIAL GROUPS

In the past, teachers have been exposed to a considerable amount of sociometry. The purpose for studying the science of human relationships and conditions is to help teachers improve students' interpersonal relations in the classroom.

One does not have to be a prominent student of sociometry to practice social grouping in the classroom; however, a teacher should know how to place students on a sociograph and then plot a sociogram before he attempts to group students for social purposes. Although teachers can get an idea of students' social preferences by observing them carefully as they choose partners for work or play, observation does not supply teachers with such valuable information as the social position of each member of the class in relation to all other members—the in-groups, cliques, and rivalries within the class. Most of all, observation will not give enough teachers pertinent information for arranging students into social groups that will improve the social conditions in the classroom.

To secure data for a sociogram, the teacher asks students to designate the students with whom they would most want to work in small groups. The students place first, second, and third choices on a piece of paper. Students should be assured that other class members will not see the names that they select.

A sociograph tabulation is a good way to begin analysis procedures. A sociograph is a simple chart with each pupil's name listed horizontally and vertically. The horizontal column is used to designate each student's first, second, and third choices, and the vertical column is used to tabulate the score each student made by being chosen.

To plot the sociogram, teachers compute the total scores made on the sociograph and use the names of the high-score students as central points. Arrows designate the students' choices. Two arrows connecting students but pointing in opposite directions designate mutual choices.

The pertinent sociometric date enables the teacher to minister to the social needs of individual students. But it is important to remember that social patterns may change dramatically during a period of a few weeks, so sociometric data should be updated periodically to be meaningful. Students should be allowed to work with partners they choose themselves before teachers begin to manipulate them to achieve desired growth.

At times, groups may be formed specifically for social goals, but having sociometric data at hand will help the teacher anytime he groups. It is especially helpful when teachers group for special purposes, such as problem solving, teacher aid, and committee work.

SPECIAL-PURPOSE GROUPS

At times, groups are formed to accomplish a specific purpose. Special-purpose groups may be based on achievement levels, interest, sociality, or needed skills. But regardless of the basis for group membership, the primary reason for forming special-purpose groups is to achieve a specific goal.

Many groups qualify for the special-purpose category. The number and types used depend on the purpose of the teacher and the needs and skills of the students. Following are descriptions of some of the most commonly used special-purpose groups:

Class Committees.   A class committee may be formed to plan, collect, and administer a class library of books, magazines, tapes, and other resources obtained from outside sources. Other class committees may involve students in class government, bulletin board planning and construction, field trip planning, interest-center constructions and maintenance, or even class and playground maintenance.

Polar Groups.   Polar groups are composed of students who are opposites in some way. Students who can comprehend the subject matter are grouped with students who are having difficulty learning. Students who have mastered a skill are grouped with students having difficulties. Students who work well with others are grouped with students who do not; or students who are dependent are grouped with students who are independent. Polar groups offer the best grouping arrangement for having students teach each other.

Pairs.   Many class activities can best be accomplished by students working in pairs. Pairs may be formed on the basis of any grouping procedure. Students grouped in pairs bridge the gap between independent study and groups of four or five, because social tasks that students and teacher must learn together are not as complex when students work in pairs.

Teacher-Aide Groups.   Teacher-aide groups aid the teacher in the classroom. Functioning as an instructional team in cooperation with the teacher, teacher-aide group members become a part of a team-teaching operation. Teacher-aide groups may also be used to construct or prepare instructional materials and to operate learning stations and centers. Serving as a teacher-aide group member is a real learning experience; however, certain students should not be relied on to perform teacher-aide duties to the extent that these duties jeopardize their roles and duties as students.

Discussion Groups.   Whole-class discussion, small-group discussion, round-table discussion, panels, symposiums, sociodramas, and strategies and techniques for organizing discussion groups and teaching discussions were discussed in detail in Chapter 1.

IMPLEMENTING INTEREST GROUPS, SOCIAL GROUPS, AND SPECIAL-PURPOSE GROUPS IN AN AMERICAN HISTORY CLASS

Introduction

History is a subject that is especially designed for creative, innovative teaching strategies and techniques. It is not a subject for passive learning whereby students are required to listen to lectures, take notes, and prepare for examinations. Students should be able to relive the past in exciting, interesting ways, using multiple resources so that they can apply what they learn to the present and future.

Although basic knowledges should apply to all students, these basic knowledges should serve as a springboard for students to range in many different directions. Students who are forced to learn history from one textbook or one lecturer may glean as much misinformation as they do factual knowledge. Students should be allowed to explore history from a wide variety of sources and situations so that they gather knowledge, develop understanding, and form generalizations from their own frame of reference.

The teaching of history offers a great opportunity for teachers to use all types of intra-class grouping procedures, but it is especially appropriate for whole-group activities, interest and social group activities, and grouping for special purposes.

Program Description

For a unit on the Second World War, the Pacific Theater, students would need basic information that could be taught best in a whole-group formation. Basic information that is necessary for all students serves as an introduction to the topic. Rarely does one find students expressing great interest in a topic before they have had an opportunity to acquaint themselves with it. A variety of techniques should be used to present the basic information in order to motivate students and to build readiness for, and interest in, the group work to follow.

One instructor conducted whole-group instruction in this manner: He announced to each class that there would be no written examination if the one hundred and twenty students in his four classes would bring souvenirs to make the room appear to be a museum for the topic to be studied.

Basic information was provided from a narrative film plus the instructor's personal experiences. His personal-experience narrative was expanded and illustrated by teacher-aide groups who prepared background decorations and drawings. Another teacher-aide group prepared a summary of basic material from three textbooks, compiling the different views and facts. Students could hear the compilation on tape, read a handout, or read the information from the original sources. The teacher-aide groups were composed of student volunteers, who prepared the materials with the teacher's direction, help, and advice.

Separate teacher-aide groups can be selected for each class or one group can have members from different classes. After the materials have been used, the best ones should be kept for the following years in case the same idea is used again. However, the materials should be revised and refined by the teacher and student groups.

Sufficient time for basic learning for all students in a whole-group formation should be provided. Some teachers like to allocate a part of each day to whole-group teaching; others prefer to use that method during the entire class time for two or three days.

Teacher-guided student planning and evaluating sessions are essential to the success of any grouping procedure. Most time will be spent on planning and evaluating when beginning and ending a topic, but some planning and evaluating should occur daily. The type of student involvement that leads toward the accomplishment of specific goals and objectives is not automatic. Students have to learn how to plan and evaluate. If the teacher doesn't teach the necessary procedures, the students may engage in irrelevant activities that do not lead to real learning.

The first planning session is vital to the success of the remaining sessions. During that session, the teacher should have students write lists of questions about the topic and then set up activities that will provide the answers to the questions. With the teacher's direction, students set up interest groups concerning the problems.

The class studying the Second World War, Pacific Theater, listed problems and formed interest groups as follows:

1. One group was formed because class members chose to research the war at sea. This group divided into two subgroups. One group was to use a large-scale map and pin-on ship models to present the strengths and weaknesses of the ships involved in the various battles. The second group was to write biographies of the major naval leaders on both sides and act out the parts of the characters on videotape.

2. A second group chose the land war and planned to use a newscast approach for reporting. The students divided into two subgroups, to describe the battles of the army and the marines. One group would report the army maneuvers and then the scene would switch to the group reporting about the marines.

3. A third group chose the problems on the home front. One subgroup was to cover governmental problems; the other, people problems. Both subgroups decided to present "You Are There" skits for reporting purposes.

The teacher consulted sociometric data to form these groups, and students agreed that a five-second time limit for getting into the groups and starting group activity was reasonable.

The students set a time limit of three days for preparation. At the end of that time, each group was allowed one day for reporting. Goals and objectives were set for each of those days, and achievement and social tasks were evaluated at the end of each day. Two final days were spent summarizing the unit and evaluating student learning. The entire unit consumed eight days of instructional time. (Although total time spent on this particular unit was almost two weeks, some teachers prefer to organize interest groups for only one or two days. The amount of time one spends in interest groups depends on the students, the situation, the subject matter, and the teacher.)

The culminating activity for this unit also served to evaluate students. Each group constructed a lottery-type cage or barrel from which questions could be drawn. With the teacher's direction and aid, the members of each group wrote eighteen questions that applied to their topic, including an equal number of questions. The instructor added to each group's barrel the fifteen questions that had been listed by the whole group during the preliminary planning session. While one student acted as monitor and evaluator at each station, groups of students rotated from barrel to barrel, drawing questions and answering them. On the last day, all the questions were put into one barrel and students came to a central location to draw and answer questions as the teacher kept score.

During whole-group activities, the teacher was planner, presenter, group leader, motivator, helper, and evaluator. In the group formation, his role was to supply pertinent information or to explain where the information could be located. He gave advice and provided direction for some groups. He asked questions and answered questions for group and individual improvement. He helped groups to organize their time and effort so that they could reach the instructional goals for the day. All the time, the teacher's personality and behavior established the tone for group and individual participation and behavior. As soon as groups formed, the teacher made a fast tour to each group, answering and asking important initial questions and establishing a businesslike atmosphere. He was careful to avoid spending too much time with any one group. The second group-to-group tour was also fast, but the teacher's questions were more penetrating, and praise and encouragement were administered to deserving students. If an individual or group was accomplishing an achievement or social task in a way that would benefit the whole class, the teacher called "time-out" to explain and to discuss the technique or point. Soon the teacher could take more time with each group; however, he was careful not to become too involved with any one group.

When the students returned to whole-group formation, they evaluated themselves and their group on the basis of achievement and performance of social tasks. Students discussed the things individual members of their subgroup had done that had helped them to achieve their goals and the things that had hindered them from accomplishing their goals as a group. Individual and group evaluations were tabulated and file reports were placed in group and individual folders. Evaluation was continual: students and teachers evaluated during the class and tabulated and filed data at the close of the day. Evaluation was comprehensive: learning goals and stated behavioral objectives formed the foundation for evaluation, and activities and learning tasks led to the fulfillment of these goals and objectives.

Although this particular example does not use the interest-station or interest-center format, the use of those grouping procedures adds variety to teaching methodology. Teachers may also wish to involve students in individual projects that they can complete outside the classroom to supplement what they have learned during class time.

SUGGESTIONS FOR EFFECTIVE GROUPING

Have a reason for grouping. If the lesson or activity can be taught just as well in a whole-group formation, why group?

Have stated goals and instructional objectives for students concerning what is to be taught and learned, and then be certain that group activities lead to the fulfillment of these goals and objectives.

Keep a whole-group formation until discipline has been established. Do not subgroup until you know students' needs, work habits, behavior patterns and abilities.

Ease into group work. Make one group a model operation before forming other groups.

Begin group work with simple problems before starting long-term group work.

Have from two to five members in a group. Any number over five usually constitutes too large a group.

Teach grouping directly by asking students to evaluate their groups. Ask group members to record and report those actions of group members that led toward the achievement of the goals of the group and those actions that hindered the group in achieving its goals. Teach appropriate roles for group members and list skills in group procedures. The listed skills may be revised into an evaluative checklist for teacher and student use.

Start and close each day's lesson with students in a whole-group formation.

Maintain a businesslike atmosphere. Have high expectations for individuals and groups.

Reward desirable behavior with deserved praise and encouragement.

Help students to set time limits for getting in and out of groups in a responsible manner. Estimated time allotments for the completion of tasks should be agreed on.

Task assessment should be practiced daily during whole-group evaluation at the close of the period. Students should not be allowed to space task responsibilities over a two- or three-day time period.

Let group membership roles emerge from the group. During evaluation, call attention to the different roles played by group members. Point out that students play many roles during group activity and that students must play different roles as the group matures in order for the group to function effectively.

Vary the types of groups. Do not become dependent on any one type. Remember that the whole class is also a group.

Be an active participant in group activities by asking questions, offering suggestions, providing aid and encouragement, and helping students with needed skills so that their product or presentation will live up to their expectations.

Have equipment, materials, and research resources ready before groups are formed.

Use students as teaching aides. Individual students may instruct group members while the teacher acts as a team leader, or teacher-aide groups may instruct in a cooperative effort with the teacher.

Provide students with accurate feedback by using audio and video tapes of group participation so that students can critique and evaluate group behavior.

Prepare evaluative instruments with students. Checklists, rating scales, achievement-task evaluations and formal tests and measuring instruments should be chosen or prepared as a class project.

Have personal evaluative conferences with individual students. Allow the student to self-evaluate using the teacher evaluation as a reference point.

Place each student in the type of group for which he is best suited.

Have students set noise level for group activity. The teacher should model the desired noise level.

Try the certificate rewards system for improving social behavior. Give certificates to groups having the highest rating for the week. Other certificates may be given to the best individual members, most improved group and class member, most creative group and class member, and so on. The most important point to remember when teachers use extrinsic rewards is that the intrinsic feelings students experience are more important than the award.

Intra-classroom grouping procedures help teachers to focus on the learner by placing students in different types of groups designed to minimize the students' differences, resulting in a more individualized teacher-learner situation. Intra-classroom grouping of students does not completely individualize instruction for students, but if it is done carefully, it is an important part of individualized instruction.

SUGGESTED READINGS

BANY, MARY A., and JOHNSON, LOIS V. *Classroom Group Behavior: Group Dynamics in Education.* New York: Macmillan Co., 1964.

CARTWRIGHT, DORWIN, and ZANDER, ALVIN. *Group Dynamics: Research and Theory.* 3rd ed. New York: Harper and Row, 1968.

GORMAN, ALFRED H. *Teachers and Learners: The Interactive Process of Education.* 2nd ed. Boston: Allyn and Bacon, 1974.

HOOVER, KENNETH H. *Learning and Teaching in the Secondary.* 3rd ed. Boston: Allyn and Bacon, 1972.

JAROLIMEK, JOHN. *Social Studies in Elementary Education.* 4th ed. New York: Macmillan Co., 1971.

LIFTON, WALTER M. *Working with Groups.* New York: John Wiley & Sons, 1966.

PHILLIPS, GERALD M. *Communication and the Small Group.* Bobbs-Merrill Co., 1973.

THELEN, HERBERT A. *Classroom Grouping for Teachability.* New York: John Wiley & Sons, 1967.

IV. Independent Study Methods

During the decade 1960–1970, use of independent study methods spread throughout the country, and whole school systems remodeled their school plants and reorganized instructional formats to accommodate independent study situations for students. Many educators espoused the tenet that independent study methodology was *the* way to individualize. Learning resource centers, automated schools, learning carrels, programmed materials and kits, television and videotaped lessons, learning packets, programmed modules, and computers became integral parts of the educator's vocabulary. Some people believed that public schools would turn completely to the use of programmed concentrated instruction; then students would learn from programmed machines and programmed materials, and teachers would be technician-teachers. In most cases, however, educators have not accepted independent study as the only means for achieving individualized instruction. But they have seen the movement as worthwhile, and they have incorporated more independent study technics and techniques into their school programs.

From this writer's point of view, independent study is an important part of individualized instruction, and teachers should certainly know how to use independent study techniques. However, it is unfair for a school system to merely add construction of learning materials to the teachers' regular teaching responsibilities. If school districts expect teachers to construct learning packets, modules, and resource centers or to become machine technicians, special provisions concerning teaching time and money should be made.

It is a misconception to think that independent study is only concerned with programmed learning. Teachers have always used independent study techniques. Any time a student is doing seatwork, whether he is studying, completing an assignment, doing workbook exercises, or solving a problem, he is accomplishing the task independently. Of course, independent study is not individualized unless the student is accomplishing a task that he is able to do.

Good teachers have always helped students to be successful in doing independent study tasks. However, because of misconceptions conderning grade standards, many teachers believe that students in a particular grade are at the same achievement level and can, therefore, be taught with the same level of subject matter. When these teachers place students in situations where they are unable to accomplish the assigned task, the results are detrimental to the individuals and to society in general. The modern independent study programs prevent this from happening because they are designed to diagnose each student and then place him at his own achievement level.

This chapter is not concerned with "traditional" independent study methods in which the same classwork, homework, and seatwork is assigned to everyone alike. It will, instead, focus on modern independent study methods whereby each student is given subject matter at his own achievement level and is allowed to progress at his own rate. Hopefully, this chapter will fulfill the following purposes:

To make educators realize that while independent study is an important facet of individualized instruction, independent study must be supplemented by other individualized methods in order to meet the needs of students

To describe an automated school, a learning resource center in action, learning packets, and programmed and comprehensive instructional modules

To describe the roles of teachers and students when independent study methods are being used

THE NEED TO BALANCE INDEPENDENT STUDY METHODS WITH OTHER METHODS

Educational theory, supported by public school teachers working daily with students, has stated that students are different in all aspects of human growth and development. They are as different in their intellectual, emotional, social, and physical development as they are in their personal appearance. Inter-differences (differences among individuals of the same chronological age) are probably greater than intra-differences (differences within the intellectual, emotional, social, and physical aspects of one individual); however, even in the intellectual domain, a student's ability to achieve fluctuates from subject to subject. Certainly, public school organization and instructional methodology should adapt to the differences of students, but this point should be made clear: *educators should strive for individualized instruction, but total, absolute individualization is neither possible nor desirable.*

While students are certainly different in many aspects of life, they are also alike in many aspects, and their likenesses should also be considered when educators organize and implement instructional programs. Students are alike in that each student needs to learn to communicate effectively; each needs to belong to a supportive social group; each needs warm interpersonal relations with teachers; each needs to examine his ideas in dialogue with others; each needs to receive praise and encouragement from other human beings, and each needs to experience situations that help him to build a positive self-concept. Therefore subject matter can sometimes be presented more effectively to all than to individuals.

Independent study methods are excellent techniques for allowing students to learn individually. They can be placed at their own achievement levels and progress at their own rates. Use of machines, learning packets, LRC areas, and instruction modules is feasible for all to a greater or lesser degree, depending on the school situation. To deny students these types of learning experiences would certainly be shortsighted.

AUTOMATED SCHOOLS

The automated-school concept is a far cry from the Little Red Schoolhouse. Classrooms are lined with glass-enclosed carrels. Each carrel is equipped with a programmed machine that the student, wearing headphones, uses to learn a variety of subjects ranging from mathematics to touch-typing. Supplementary materials, shelved at a central location, are checked in and out by students. All the curriculum materials are programmed, and reading and mathematics analyzers diagnose students' difficulties and prescribe a remedial program to correct them.

Students have a home-base seating and desk arrangement in which they are able to engage in recreational reading, personal conferences with teachers and aides, group activities, and general class meetings. During physical education, art, and music periods, students in group formations learn to use special equipment, instructed by specialist-teachers.

Formal and informal evaluative instruments are an important, integral part of the program, for teachers must be able to provide the correct materials for the individual student. An individualized checklist is used to report student progress. Goals and objectives are listed on the report form, together with tasks that fulfill the goals and objectives. The report form gives the parent information such as the student's rate of progress in relation to objectives and goals, as well as pertinent information regarding the student's social, emotional, and physical development. Comparative data is shared with parents during parent-counselor conferences so that parents may plan for their child's future.

The automated-school movement has influenced educators to use teaching machines in practical and strategic instructional programs. Practical teaching machines are also being used in the regular classroom to a greater degree as an adjunct to other types of individualized teaching methods. The automated-school movement has had a tremendous impact on entrepreneurs. They have manufactured machines and machine packets, programmed materials, and supplementary materials by the storefull, and all these products are available to educators.

Even if the necessary funds could be appropriated to finance automated schools, the automated-school movement could never become popular in the United States. This is true primarily because machines can only provide individualization; they cannot provide personalization. And personalized instruction is just as important as individualized instruction.

LEARNING RESOURCE CENTERS

A learning resource center is essentially a miniature automated school within a school. Usually, a large area is provided to house teaching machines, individual carrels, seminar rooms, all types of learning packages, programmed modules, various kinds of media, and supplementary materials. Personnel to operate the learning resource center usually in-

clude a director, technician-teachers, aides, clerks, and
student-helpers. Volunteers from the community serve as
technicians, aides, and clerks in some situations, but key
personnel should be employed if the center is to run
efficiently and smoothly.

Although students and teachers may use the center in
many ways, the usual procedure is for teachers to send or
take students there individually or in groups to complete
tasks independently. In a typical learning resource center,
one would see students of all ages and abilities using teaching
machines at individual carrels. Some of these machines provide instant feedback. Other students would be using media
and supplementary materials to complete a small-group
assignment, while still others might be meeting with a
technician-teacher or an aide to prepare for a planned seminar. All of these experiences would help students to complete
independent study assignments appropriate to their individual needs.

Private entrepreneurs supply the LRC areas with
machines, lessons, individualized programs, programmed
modules, subject-matter packets with lessons using media,
and even diagnostic instruments for ascertaining the
student's achievement levels. In many cases, however, much
of the software is developed by teachers and students to fit
their local situations. When teachers and students participate
in the development of materials, they should receive special
instruction and help so that the software will follow the same
format and conform to high quality standards. Program developers must have special talents; every person is not a
software specialist, so special committees should be formed
for developing materials, and time and money should be
provided to allow program developers to produce outstanding
products.

If a learning resource area is to become an important
part of the total school program, teachers, administrators,
and students must believe in its worth. Preservice and in-
service sessions should involve students and teachers in experiences with the center so that they may feel competent
and comfortable when using it. Students and teachers should
help plan the organization and administration of the center,
and constant evaluative feedback from students and teachers
will help the center personnel to analyze and evaluate the
center constantly so that its services may improve continuously.

The LRC must not disintegrate into a place that is used merely to house remedial and enrichment programs. The center should be a place where all students can independently study tasks that are closely interwoven with the total instructional program. Students should be held accountable for independent learning, and LRC lessons should be considered during total evaluation. Allowing the center to become a place where teachers send students just to get them out of the room, away from something else, will destroy the effectiveness of the center. Centers that encourage teachers to bring their students seem to have better coordination among students, teachers, and LRC personnel than centers where children come alone.

The LRC movement can be only as effective as the people involved. There is a danger that LRC areas will resemble some of the media centers of the past; that is, expensive equipment and materials will gather dust while teachers continue to use traditional methodology.

LEARNING PACKETS

A group of six teachers employed to teach students in grades one, two, and three joined forces to construct packets containing the phonics knowledges and skills their students would need. A series of one hundred "talk-along packets" (exercises with audiotaped directions) were developed containing lessons on every facet of phonics from beginning consonants to reading sentence accents. The packets were cataloged, filed, and placed in a central location, readily accessible to students and teachers. Pretests and post-tests were included in each packet. From these tests, four achievement level pretests were constructed.

At the beginning of the school term, pretests were administered to students; then checklist charts were compiled for each student, indicating which packets the student needed. As an adjunct to their regular language arts program, teachers adapted phonics packets to individual needs and capabilities and allowed students to work on packets at a specified time each day.

The students took their packets to listening stations and became occupied with their particular tasks. Teachers moved from one individual to another, encouraging students and helping those who were experiencing difficulties. The teachers noted what difficulties the students were experiencing so that needed-skills groups could be formed at another time for teacher-directed instruction. A businesslike atmosphere prevailed, for students were expected to make good use of their time, according to their individual capabilities. Students checked their own post-tests with the help of teachers, who rotated the checking responsibility. Files were updated during a personal conference between the student and his regular home-base teacher.

Learning packets are subject matter oriented, but individualization occurs because students' needs are diagnosed and the students are placed in situations where they can experience success. A number of students are able to work independently at the same time on different tasks. Special precaution should be exercised to be sure that the diagnosis of a student's knowledge and needs is accurate, and that the student is given appropriate packet materials. To construct packets and then require all students to complete all packet materials in sequence is a violation of the meaning and purpose of individualized instruction.

Packets may be used in team-teaching situations, in LRC areas, or in a regular classroom setting. The development and use of programs of this sort vastly improve the learning situation for students. But there is a danger that an overemphasis on packet construction and packet teaching may nullify its value. Packets should be used in conjunction with other methods so that all the children's needs may be met.

PROGRAMMED INSTRUCTION MODULES

A module is a unit of learning theoretically constructed according to the tenets of behavioral psychology. A programmed instructional module is a self-contained unit, written in behavioral terminology, that is a part of a total instructional program.

Although the terminology used in each module may differ, most programmed modules contain seven parts:

1. *The rationale* is a statement of justification for including the module as a part of the instructional system. The rationale is based on theory, logic, and practical experi-

ence, and is written in a clear, precise manner to convey the importance and relevancy of the goals and objectives of the module.

2. *The prerequisites* state what the student must have already accomplished in order to begin this module.

3. *The objectives* are stated in learner terminology. That is, the performance criteria are specified for students, as is the level for successful completion. The key word in behavioral objective is *behavior.* Each written behavioral objective must have a verb that specifies an observable behavior or performance.

4. *A preassessment* allows student and teacher to gauge the learner's competence in light of the stated objectives. On the basis of the preassessment data, a student may have to complete other modules before attempting this one, he may receive credit without completing the modular activities, or he may focus on certain specified areas of the module.

5. *The enabling activities* for a programmed instruction module are self-instructional and follow the programmed book or media format. Therefore, students can complete the activities and fulfill the performance objectives independently. Samples of objectives are included in the next section. (For a detailed explanation of how to write performance objectives, refer to Robert Mager's book on preparing behavioral objectives.)[1] Materials for enabling activities make up the bulk of a programmed instructional module, and their preparation is time consuming.

6. *The postassessment* measures the student's ability to meet the objectives of the module. Successful performance on the post-test represents the completion of the module. Unsuccessful performance leads to a recycling process through remedial activities, including other instructional techniques.

7. *Remediation* explains what the student must do if he was unable to complete the postassessment satisfactorily.

A programmed instructional module is a solitary system operating independently within the framework of many systems that lead to global goals and objectives. The module has a built-in capacity to perform individualization tasks such as diagnosing, prescribing, teaching, evaluating, and recycling, which are tasks the teacher has to perform when using learning packets. Both teacher and students know the

---

[1] Robert Frank Mager, *Preparing Instructional Objectives* (San Francisco: Fearon Publishers, 1962).

precise learning objectives, and the learner accepts responsibility for meeting the objectives and expects to be held accountable in each case.

Well-constructed modules offer teachers a finite alternative for individualizing instruction; instead of merely talking about the ways to individualize, programmed instruction modules involve students and teachers in a specific system for individualizing. However, it is often difficult to write explicit objectives in behavioral terms.

Professionals must also overcome some other barriers if modules are to become a major vehicle for individualizing instruction. The most prominent barriers include teachers' belief in mass-teaching methods, fear of change, and a lack of effective in-service programs for teachers.

COMPREHENSIVE INSTRUCTION MODULES

A comprehensive modular system is more than an independent study method, because within the framework of modular construction any teaching method may become an alternate learning route for a student. The system is independent to the degree that students matriculate through modules on the basis of independent decisions. A comprehensive modular system can be the organizational format for a particular school or school system.

The parts of the comprehensive module are the same as those of programmed modules, except for one major difference—the enabling activities are changed to alternate learning routes. The difference can be illustrated by first presenting a programmed module on handwriting positions, then pointing out how that module can be changed to a comprehensive module.

L. r. 001.00 HANDWRITING MODULE
(PROGRAMMED INSTRUCTION)

Correct Positions for Cursive Writing

RATIONALE

In order to master the skills necessary for such sports as tennis or golf, the player must learn the correct way to hold the racket or club and the correct placement of the body for making the various strokes. Handwriting skills are learned the same way. When you learn the correct way to hold your pen, the correct sitting position, the correct paper position, and the correct way to write cursively at the chalkboard, your chances for writing well and comfortably are improved. The purpose of this module is to teach you the correct positions for cursive writing, and then to let you demonstrate the positions as you prepare to write.

OBJECTIVES

1. Whether the student is right-handed or left-handed, he will demonstrate the correct procedure for holding a pen and placing his paper for cursive writing.
2. The student will demonstrate the correct sitting position for cursive writing. (Right-handers demonstrate right-handedness, and left-handers demonstrate left-handedness.)
3. The student will demonstrate the correct position for writing at the chalkboard. (Right-handers demonstrate right-handedness; left-handers demonstrate left-handedness.)

PREREQUISITES

The student must have completed all manuscript modules and the readiness-for-cursive-writing modules.

PREASSESSMENT

The student will demonstrate correct positions for cursive writing at the writing desk and chalkboard.

ENABLING ACTIVITIES

1. Read and listen to "A Talk-Along Handwriting Plan";[2] practice the correct procedures until you feel comfortable using them.
2. Examine the charts and descriptions in your textbook describing correct positions for cursive handwriting. Practice the correct procedures on the position frames in the corner of the classroom.

POSTASSESSMENT

The student will describe the correct positions for cursive writing at the writing desk and the chalkboard. The student will demonstrate the correct positions for cursive writing at the writing desk and the chalkboard.

REMEDIATION

If necessary, the student will repeat enabling activity No. 1 or No. 2 with an assigned peer or teaching aide.

---

[2] George Ray Musgrave, *A Talk-Along Handwriting Instruction Book* (Houston, Tex.: D. Armstrong Co., 1973), pp. 49–53.

A comprehensive module would include the following changes:

ALTERNATE LEARNING ROUTES (substituted for *Enabling Activities*)

1. During a classroom instruction period, the teacher will display large wall charts depicting the correct positions for cursive writing at the writing desk and the chalkboard. He will point out the correct procedures and then distribute desk models for students to complete showing the correct procedures.

2. During a class demonstration, two students (one right-handed, and one left-handed) will demonstrate the correct positions for cursive writing at the writing desk and the chalkboard, while the teacher points out the correct procedure.

3. Working in groups of four, students will demonstrate the correct positions for cursive writing at the writing desk and chalkboard to the other group members while explaining the positions in detail.

4. Enabling activity No. 1 of programmed module.

5. Enabling activity No. 2 of programmed module.

6. The student will read any handwriting text of his choice and practice the correct positions for cursive writing at the writing desk and chalkboard.

7. The student will devise his own procedure for learning the correct positions for cursive writing at the writing desk and chalkboard. He will discuss the plan with the teacher before proceeding.

REMEDIATION

Recycle students through alternate routes with teacher support.

There are different avenues of thought concerning the sequencing of alternate routes. Some module writers believe in independent routes, with each route enabling the student to reach the objectives of the module. Other writers believe that the routes should be interdependent, and that students should experience all the routes in order to meet the objectives. The alternate routes in this example mini-module were written to help the student select the route or routes that best suit his learning style preference. However, each route is independent and has the capacity to prepare the student to attain the module objectives.

Programmed modules used as an adjunct to other methods of teaching can be a part of any teaching situation, but comprehensive modules require more teaching personnel. Team-teaching situations provide teachers with all the ingredients necessary for implementing comprehensive modular instruction. Open-area buildings provide a physical arrangement that is conducive to all forms of individualized instruction. Many new schools have plants that are designed to promote individualized instruction, but good programs also exist in outmoded buildings. The main impetus for any program is not necessarily buildings, equipment, materials, or even the programs. Altruistic, competent, dedicated people are necessary!

A systemic approach to curriculum development using modules as units of learning may become a viable movement if educators adhere to these necessary procedures:

1. There should be in-depth preservice and in-service educational experiences for educators, with university and public school personnel joining the professional organizations and public as team members in a comprehensive cooperative program. The relationships must be on equal terms, with each group willing to relinquish a certain amount of autonomy to accomplish team goals.
2. Instructional modules must be evaluated continuously by team members of the school community. Modules should be modified, refined, updated, or deleted according to well-defined evaluative criteria.
3. Programmed modules should be supplemented by other methods of teaching.
4. Systemic curricular development demands a considerable amount of expertise, time, money, and effort toward a common goal. Educators should allow for preparation time before instituting a modular instructional format. An impossible situation occurs when participants attempt to develop a new program while they are still implementing the old program.

SUGGESTIONS FOR MAKING INDEPENDENT STUDY MORE EFFECTIVE

The development of an independent-study instructional component—including a guiding philosophy, instructional objectives, scope and sequence descriptions, and evaluative instruments and tests—should precede the procurement of teaching machines and materials.

Commercial instructional materials are usually more expertly prepared, but these materials may lack relevancy for local program objectives, and programs and materials may become outdated quickly. If independent study is a popular technique for a particular building or school system, operational budgets must include expenditures for teachers and technicians to engage in cooperative program-development projects that do not interfere with instructional responsibilities. Weekends, evening hours, summertime periods, and specified times during the school day may be designated as program-development time for which teachers and technicians receive adequate compensation.

A technician to handle minor machine repairs should be on the scene, and the school district should also employ a major repairman. If machines have to be sent away to be repaired and teachers wait weeks for their return, students and teachers will lose interest in independent study.

A school system should not adopt programmed instructional materials without letting the teachers ascertain whether the program is relevant to their instructional philosophy.

Teach students to work independently as a whole-class unit before allowing them to move to learning stations on their own. Make the structured situation for independent study a successful operation before attempting independent study at stations.

Ease into the use of independent-study carrels or learning resource centers. Allow a few students to operate independently at first. Make their experience a model operation by allowing all class members to help construct a checklist of procedures that make independent study successful for students. Then, allow the whole class to evaluate the model operation. Gradually increase the number of students working independently, letting the class perceive independent study as a responsibility and a reward, until the whole class is participating. Occasionally, a student may not be ready to operate and learn independently, and he must be brought back into a more structured situation for learning.

An overemphasis on independent study will lead to boredom and aimless activity for many students. No matter how good the machine or program may be, the interpersonal rewards that result when students learn from a teacher and with each other are also necessary for a well-rounded instructional program.

Time limits for moving to and from learning stations should be agreed on by students and teacher, and a time limit for completing the independent study task should also be negotiated by student and teacher. To make a long-term contract with a student and then allow him to proceed at his own pace may instigate procrastination.

For each independent study task, students should be held accountable for either a written or an oral product.

A system of individual and group rewards may be useful for some teachers. This is especially true for teachers attempting to get an independent study operation off the ground. Students may be rewarded for being the best independent study group, the best independent study student, or the most improved independent study group or student. A student might also be rewarded for being the most considerate or for producing the best product. Students seem to be most satisfied with a system of rewards when the students help to formulate the criteria for rewards and when a number of rewards are given so that all students have a chance to receive one.

Types of rewards for elementary school children include special privileges and duties, such as being office helper, room helper, plant or animal guardian, and host or hostess for visitors; having free class time; having stars displayed by their name on a bulletin board; getting special stars or things to wear; and being allowed certain playground privileges. Secondary school students prefer exemptions from assignments and examinations, free time, extra grade points, and game time selections as rewards. The rewards given at any level are not as important as the interpersonal feelings between teacher and students.

Begin and end each independent study task with a whole-group formation. During the whole-group session at the beginning of the period, planning that is essential to everyone may be accomplished. Time limits are established, assessment procedures for independent study products are made clear, criteria for the behavioral checklist are explained, and individual questions that are valuable to all are answered. When students disperse for independent study time, teachers should be on the scene, answering questions, giving aid and encouragement, observing, evaluating, and supervising the entire operation. If teachers send students to independent study stations where a learning resource specialist supervises students, learning gaps and behavioral problems may occur, because the teacher is not a part of the independent study operation.

When students return from their independent study assignments at the close of the study period, each student meets with the teacher to evaluate his product, which in some instances the machine or program helped him to do. Each student and the teacher have agreed on a seat activity that the student will engage in while he waits for this short personal conference. (A short conference of three to five minutes is preferable to a long one.) At the close of each conference, the teacher records the results on the proper form and files the information in the student's evaluation folder.

Teachers should model the proper noise level by talking in quiet, clear voice tones and by using media and noisy activities in the proper places.

Remember that students have different learning styles. Some students are independent learners who enjoy learning alone, while others are dependent learners who enjoy learning from and with others. Even in independent learning situations, teachers are able to accommodate the different learning styles by assisting dependent students at learning stations and allowing students to complete tasks in pairs or small groups occasionally.

Although all groups must be taught to operate independently, one group may become independent in a short period of time while another group needs much more time. This statement is also true about individuals. To ask students to become independent learners before they are ready may result in chaos.

SUGGESTED READINGS

BOGGS, DAVID W., and BUFFS, EDWARD G., eds. *Independent Study: Bold New Venture.* Bloomington: Indiana University Press, 1965.

DRESSEL, PAUL L., and THOMPSON, MARY MAGDALA. *Independent Study: A New Interpretation of Concepts, Practices and Problems.* San Francisco: Jossey-Bass, Publishers, 1973.

Fund For The Advancement of Education, The. *Four Case Studies of Programmed Instruction.* New York, 1964.

GLASSER, ROBERT. *Teaching Machines and Programmed Learning.* Washington, D.C.: National Education Association of the United States, 1965.

LYSAUGHT, JEROME P., and WILLIAMS, CLARENCE M. *Guide to Programmed Instruction.* New York: John Wiley & Sons, 1963.

SKINNER, B. F. *The Technology of Teaching.* New York: Appleton-Century-Crofts, 1968.

THOMPSON, JAMES J. *Instructional Communication.* New York: Van Nostrand Reinhold Co., 1969.

V. Individual Differences: Practitioner-Theorist Confrontations

Differences in Innate Ability to Accomplish Scholastic Tasks

Differences in Rate of Achievement

Differences in Language Ability

Differences in Creative Ability

Differences in Physical Development and Rate of Growth

Differences in Personal and Social Adjustment

Differences in Home Background

Differences in Attitudes and Beliefs

Educational Implications

The acceptance of the concept that important differences exist within the individual student and that even greater differences exist among different students is a prerequisite for accepting instruction that focuses on the learner. Differences within the individual are usually referred to as intra-individual differences, and differences among students of comparable age and grade level are defined as inter-individual differences. This chapter is concerned with developing the following thesis:

Individual differences exist to such an extent that focus-on-the-learner strategies and procedures are necessary and desirable.

Variations that exist within the individual student and among different school children of the same age and grade level have been the subject of systematic research for almost a century. Because both theorist and practitioner are aware of individual differences, progress has been made toward understanding them. Individualized instruction in its many forms constitutes a viable educational movement in the United States for increasing knowledge of such differences.

Do practitioners in the public schools and theorists involved in research at colleges and universities have similar beliefs concerning individual differences? Let us assume that from a large number of outstanding teachers in a particular school system, a committee of six is chosen to draft statements concerning individual differences. Simultaneously, a select group of six educational theorists is chosen and charged with the same task. The groups meet in separate rooms at the same location to reach a consensus on beliefs about individual differences. Each committee is to write a brief summary statement covering its beliefs concerning each of these topics:

Differences in Innate Ability to Accomplish Scholastic Tasks
Differences in Rate of Achievement
Differences in Language Ability

Differences in Creative Ability
Differences in Physical Development and Rate of Growth
Differences in Personal and Social Adjustment
Differences in Home Background
Differences in Attitudes and Beliefs
Educational Implications

Each topic is to be considered with regard to both intra- and inter-differences. At the close of the conferences, the two groups meet together to discuss the implications that these differences have for education.

The committees follow the proposed topical guidelines and present the following original statements.

DIFFERENCES IN INNATE ABILITY
TO ACCOMPLISH SCHOLASTIC TASKS

PRACTITIONERS *(Intra-differences) Our experience in teaching students has caused us to believe that an individual is born with a general mental capacity to perform scholastic tasks. But a person does not inherit innate abilities as one complete unit of identical elements. A student may be quick and perceptive in an arithmetic class, but not so able in spelling. Certainly, individual abilities vary considerably from one content area to another. Our consensus is that if we had the opportunity to teach students on a one-to-one basis, the level of appropriate subject matter would spread across grade levels for almost every student. If we placed the student at the same level in each subject, the content would be too easy for the student in some subjects and too difficult in others. The evidence seems to prove that a student with a high degree of ability in mathematics is not necessarily endowed with a high degree of ability in English or science.*

THEORISTS *(Intra-differences) Most scholars agree that a general factor of intelligence is operative in all situations; however, research in measurements of intellectual capacity and studies of human brain structure have indicated conclusively that a student does not possess equal abilities in all areas. Historically, intelligence tests have been developed to measure primary abilities. Some scholars claim to have identified over 150 primary abilities. Recognition of the biological basis for the theory that there are interdependent performance chambers in the brain, with each part responsible for one type of performance, prompts us to agree that while an individual may be generally bright or dull, his innate abilities to accomplish scholastic tasks vary from subject to subject.*

PRACTITIONERS *(Inter-differences)   Students do not possess equal abilities to accomplish scholastic tasks. Regardless of how students are grouped, a teacher quickly realizes that students have varying abilities to accomplish tasks in the classroom. We believe that IQ scores can be accepted as indicators of students' innate abilities to learn. A wide range of difference in students' IQ scores will prevail in any regular classroom, and we agree that even when students with similar IQ scores are grouped together, there still exists a wide range of difference in the students' mental abilities. In all our combined years of teaching, we have taught rapid learners and slow learners, but most of our experiences have been with learners between these extremes. Each individual inherits special genes that make up various parts of the brain, and each student has a different capacity to accomplish scholastic tasks.*

THEORISTS *(Inter-differences)   Studies of school children in all countries have consistently revealed that students do not possess equal abilities for approaching scholastic tasks. Grade-level IQ scores ranging from 40 to 170 have been reported. About 1 to 2 percent of the world population may be designated intellectual geniuses, while approximately 60 percent would be designated normal in the range of IQ scores. Students scoring between 80 and 90 are usually considered to be dull, and students with IQ scores below 70 are considered mentally defective for educational purposes. Research evidence supports the belief that students' innate abilities to accomplish scholastic tasks differ considerably from student to student.*

DIFFERENCES IN RATE OF ACHIEVEMENT

PRACTITIONERS *(Intra-differences)   There is a general age-time sequence in patterns of achievement; however, each child has his own unique age-time sequence pattern. The general tendency has been to expect students with high achievement abilities to succeed always. However, students are affected by many factors, such as personal motivation, study habits, and relations with teachers, peers, and parents. Each student follows an independent achievement route, which is not determined by ability alone. If we were to select a high school graduating class and inspect each graduate's public school achievement records, the subject matter achievement profile from subject to subject would show peaks and valleys rather than a horizontal plain.*

THEORISTS *(Intra-differences) We agree that the rate of achievement within an individual is not constant. A student's achievement rate will vary from subject to subject, even when the subjects are closely related, such as reading and spelling. A student should be expected to approach the numerous skills and concepts in a particular subject with varying rates of interest. He should be expected to work at varying rates of speed within any reasonable time period rather than conforming to the preconceived pattern designated as normal or average in popular thinking.*

PRACTITIONERS *(Inter-differences) In any classroom, there are great differences between the students' rates of achievement in scholastic tasks. Anyone who has spent time in the classroom realizes that there is a wide range of differences in reading achievement, study skills, and skills in organizing and using time and materials. These skills are acquired individually. The acquisition is not a group project, but comes through individual experiences in and out of school. Although there are commonalities among students' rates of achievement, the range of variability in any classroom requires teachers to teach subject matter on different levels of difficulty.*

THEORISTS *(Inter-differences) Differences in rate of achievement of students in any regular classroom are great. For example, a fourth-grade class will likely contain students capable of achieving at an eighth-grade level and students only capable of achieving at the first-grade level. About 60 percent of the class will be achieving from 4.0 grade level to 5.0 grade level. The remainder of the class will be above or below grade level. The mechanized teacher who attempts to teach subject matter on a particular grade level will present content that is too easy for a number of students and too difficult for others. Grouping students administratively narrows the variability range among students in a classroom, but achievement grouping does not erase student differences to the extent that mass instruction becomes any more appropriate. Levels of difficulty and variations in style, approaches, and student performance are elements to be dealt with in preparing learning experiences for any group of students.*

DIFFERENCES IN LANGUAGE ABILITY

PRACTITIONERS *(Intra-differences)   There are many facets to the development of language proficiencies. A person may have the facility to listen or to speak at a certain level, but his ability to write or to read might be at a much lower level. There are a number of different abilities involved in the development of reading, and an individual might be capable in one skill and deficient in another. Language proficiencies vary within a person according to the language tool being used and the level of proficiency that is required.*

THEORISTS *(Intra-differences)   The language a student uses fluctuates according to the situation and the particular role he is playing. A student talking to a group of peers may use a peer vocabulary, but when he talks to teachers he may communicate with a vocabulary that will cause him to be successful at school. To accurately assess a particular student's language ability, one would need to sample language capabilities at various locations as the student interacts with different individuals and groups. Because of changes in environmental and educational conditions, students' language abilities may improve dramatically or, in some cases, deteriorate considerably. Language is forever changing, and an individual's capacity to use the language that is appropriate to the occasion is ever changing also.*

PRACTITIONERS *(Inter-differences)   Language differences are clearly evident when children enter school. Home and neighborhood environmental patterns influence children to adopt the language patterns of family and friends. Each student is influenced by a different language environment, and in many instances, there are extreme differences between languages used to communicate at home and those used to communicate at school. Many students have limited experience with the type of language used at school because they speak an entirely different language at home; therefore, their ability to understand and to speak English must be in terms of the language they already use to communicate with others. Differences between home and school dialects may be severe enough to cause language difficulties for students attempting to adjust to school language.*

Even when family and neighborhood language patterns are similar to those used and taught at school, all students do not develop language faculties at the same time and rate. Many students have speech and hearing difficulties that retard their abilities to communicate effectively.

One does not need to be a teacher to know that students' listening, speaking, writing, and reading vocabularies differ considerably at any age or grade level. The ability to verbalize effectively and the ability to observe and to listen vary from one individual to another. Teachers at all grade levels need to provide many opportunities for students to communicate at school, using all forms of communication.

THEORISTS *(Inter-differences) Each student has language abilities that are different from any other individual. Even children from the same home environment have different language abilities. The firstborn child is usually accelerated in language development when compared to other siblings in the family. Sex-difference studies concerning language development indicate that girls' language abilities are superior to boys' abilities in the same families. If children reared in the same home environment have differing language abilities, then the variability of students' language abilities in a typical classroom where the children's hereditary and environmental backgrounds are different would be considerable.*

Socioeconomic conditions are a factor in language development in the public schools. Students from middle and upper socioeconomic families have superior language abilities that help them to succeed at school. Students whose language backgrounds are different from those required in the public schools have language handicaps that cause such students to experience difficulties as they attempt to adjust to school language requirements.

DIFFERENCES IN CREATIVE ABILITY

PRACTITIONERS *(Intra-differences) A student may have special creative talents in one area of the public school curriculum that do not carry over into other areas. For example, he may be creative in art while his writing style is pedantic and conforming. Creative ability, in this instance, may be described as a specific talent rather than a general quality.*

Students may have a special creative talent within the framework of a subject that is not apparent in all phases of the subject. For example, a student may exhibit a great amount of creativity for composing songs, but his creative talent deserts him when he attempts to arrange musical scores. Even if a student reveals creative ability in a variety of situations, the quality of creativity is usually greater in one area than in another.

THEORISTS *(Intra-differences)   Research has shown that the act of creating is individualistic. That is, what a student creates may be original and unique to him without being the same to others. If parents and teachers stress individuality, students' abilities to create will grow, and creative abilities within an individual at one developmental stage will be different from those at another age and time.*

Although everyone is born with a certain amount of creative ability, the amount of creative ability he will eventually display is based on his experiences as he grows up. A student's past experiences with creative situations and persons will affect the way he reacts to situations and teachers during the school day. The creative ability exhibited will fluctuate according to the atmosphere the teacher creates and the teaching methods used.

PRACTITIONERS *(Inter-differences)   Every student has a certain amount of creative ability, but creative abilities vary from student to student. There is as much difference between students' creative abilities as there is between their intellectual abilities. As we get to know students intimately during a school term, we learn which ones exhibit such thinking qualities as originality, uniqueness, imagination, and flexibility of thought and action. This type of person is a different type from the convergent thinker, who follows intellectual pursuits that make him successful in the traditional school setting.*

We observe students who are creative writers, artists, inventors, musicians, mathematicians, speakers or designers. Not only does each student have a different specific area of creativity, but he also has unique creative qualities that make him different from every other creative individual.

The enhancement of creative thinking processes has been neglected in the public schools in the past. Our society needs creative people, and creative students should be rewarded to the same extent as students who exhibit intellectual proficiencies.

THEORISTS *(Inter-differences)   Standardized tests have been constructed to help measure students' creative abilities. According to these tests, students vary considerably in their creative abilities. Special tests in art, music, mathematics, and creative writing have been designed to help select students who are creative in those areas. These tests indicate that students who are judged to be creative in the specific area tested do not have the same creative abilities in other fields. There are extreme differences between groups of students who possess creative abilities and those who do not, but differences also exist among creative individuals.*

Much of the time, the creative individual has not been acccepted in the public schools merely because he is different. He does not identify with the teachers' goals as the intellectually gifted student does. Teachers and students reject a student who tries to perform in original, different, and sometimes unusual ways. Creative teachers who use a variety of methods and techniques help creative students to attain better learning results.

DIFFERENCES IN PHYSICAL DEVELOPMENT AND RATE OF GROWTH

PRACTITIONERS *(Intra-differences) We are aware of the stages of human growth and development. We accept the theory that at certain chronological ages students are alike in many ways. Yet, we believe that each individual has a unique pattern of physical development and rate of growth. Physical competencies change as the individual grows. The boy or girl who has been too small to participate in some sports becomes a totally different part of the scene after a year or even a summer of growth. The tall, awkward student gains skill and coordination, not only increasing his physical prowess, but altering his self-concept as well. Differences in muscular coordination and physical status are not static, and the individual's academic growth, emotional and social stability, and self-concept will vary in accordance with his unique growth cycle.*

THEORISTS *(Intra-differences) All human beings progress through predictable stages of growth and development, but they do not develop to the same extent or at the same rate. Each student's growth rate and maturation rate are influenced by heredity and environmental factors. The distance that an individual deviates from the mean for his age and grade group fluctuates as he matures.*

PRACTITIONERS *(Inter-differences) We are aware of tremendous differences in physical development and range of growth among students. As we watch students on the playground or observe them in classes, it is obvious to us*

*that students of the same age exhibit different heights,
weights, shapes, muscular coordination, and facial appearances. There is a wide range of difference in students'
abilities to accomplish physical tasks. Physical differences
are so obvious that we cannot expect the same attainment
from each student, even though they all play the same
games at times.*

THEORISTS *(Inter-differences)   Differences in physical growth
rate are apparent among newborn babies. Nurses and doctors note differences not only in size and shape, but also in
eating, moving, and noticing objects or light. With the
passage of time, these physical differences become more
numerous and definitive. Although there is a degree of
likeness in a common age group, there are differences in
physical development and rate of growth, based on biological inheritance and environmental influences. We agree
that differences in this area are as apparent as differences
in physical appearance.*

DIFFERENCES IN PERSONAL AND
SOCIAL ADJUSTMENT

PRACTITIONERS *(Intra-differences)   We believe that while
there is some consistency in the personal and social adjustment of an individual to life situations, the ways in
which a student behaves in different situations are numerous and unpredictable. A student's adjustment to a particular peer group or teacher at a certain age or time is not
predictive of how he will react at another time or in a
different situation. Living in today's world with its tensions and frustrations precludes any absolutes in a
student's personal and social adjustment status.*

THEORISTS *(Intra-differences)   Personal and social differences exist in individual students as they assume various
roles in their society. A particular student may have different problems adjusting to siblings at home than he has
adjusting to other students at school. The student may
behave quite differently from class to class, depending on
such factors as the teacher, the group of classmates, and
the subject matter. The individual's personal and social
adjustment is dependent on his particular society as well
as the role that he assumes in that environment.*

PRACTITIONERS *(Inter-differences)   Students differ in their
degree of adjustment to other persons in their society.*

Personal adjustment is a prerequisite for social adjustment. Personal adjustment and getting along with others are critical elements for a student's success in school, as well as in every other area of his life. Our goal as teachers is to be personally and socially adjusted ourselves so that we can accept students unconditionally in the personal and social realm.

THEORISTS *(Inter-differences) Differences in personal and social adjustment are probably due more to environmental influences than to hereditary factors. Since each individual interacts with a different social environment, he is different personally and socially from every other being. Individual adjustment depends upon the person's perception of himself. A positive perception of self influences an individual to act positively toward others. But the identification of an individual's true personality traits is sometimes difficult, because some people are not able to communicate their feelings. What is meant to be a smile by the sender may be interpreted as a smirk or a sneer by the receiver. There is no doubt that complex and important differences are abundant in the areas of personal and social adjustment.*

DIFFERENCES IN HOME BACKGROUND

PRACTITIONERS *(Intra-differences) Each student has a different situation and set of experiences in his home that make him a unique individual. The number of people in the family, the kinds of interaction among them, the size of the home, and the position of the family unit in the community account for differences within the individual before he enters a school setting. The attitudes and values of the home become evident in the behavior of the student in the school setting. If the home provides security in family strength or a field of continuous conflict for the student, the effects are noticeable in his daily activities in the classroom or on the playground. Secure adults accept the uniqueness of personality as a significant factor to be considered in preparing any segment of the educational process.*

THEORISTS *(Intra-differences) All other differences within the individual that have been described are affected by his home background. His perception of himself is a product of his position within his family, as well as physical factors in the home environment. In addition, his increasing*

*awareness of differences between his home world and the
school world results in increasingly complex role playing
as he adjusts to the differences. Acceptance in the school
setting increases his potential for becoming a rounded
person.*

PRACTITIONERS *(Inter-differences)   Differences between students are often related to differences in the students' home
backgrounds. Teachers tend to note the home background
factor when they analyze problems in the school setting,
but they are able to do very little to influence the student's
home environment. However, some teachers encourage and
support all students, individually and in large groups, to
develop adequate patterns of behavior in the school setting
to help to counter influences from negative home environments.*

*Professionals who do not make value judgments but
rather help the student to develop his personal and peer
group identity contribute to positive individual growth
among students in the learning situation.*

THEORISTS *(Inter-differences)   In the past, differences among
students from different backgrounds have been ignored,
with negative results for the students. Greater attention to
problems of children from the lower socioeconomic levels
has resulted in a move to assist them in becoming an
integral part of their peer group. Their differences are
being viewed as strengths to build on, rather than weaknesses to overcome. Teachers become a part of the solution
the student seeks, rather than an element of new conflict.
But many schools are far from successful in their methods
for attaining this goal. More attention to human needs is
necessary from the school system and personnel and in the
curriculum. Administrators and teachers must develop
greater understanding and professional competence in
creating and maintaining a fairer school climate for each
student.*

DIFFERENCES IN ATTITUDES AND BELIEFS

PRACTITIONERS *(Intra-differences)   Attitudes and beliefs do
not exist in a vacuum. An infant is not born with either
good or bad attitudes toward school, nor does he believe
that he is incapable of learning. Attitudes and beliefs are
formed by one's interaction with significant others in one's
life, including family, peers, and teachers.*

Because attitudes and beliefs are formed by others, we

believe that an individual's attitudes are changed as he is influenced by people who are significant to him. Students' attitudes toward school are different in certain classes because the students define the situations differently. Beliefs can also be changed. What a student believes one day may be changed through experience, so that he may believe something entirely different the next day. Beliefs about self are more resistant to change, but what happens to the student at school is important to the development of self-concept.

THEORISTS *(Intra-differences)   Individuals demonstrate different attitudes and beliefs, depending on where they are. Students will not hesitate to espouse certain attitudes and beliefs in public, which they will only admit to others at home, or even deny them altogether. A student may display broad-minded and tolerant attitudes and beliefs at school or church, but his private thoughts and actions may be something else entirely.*

Attitudes and beliefs differ within an individual according to their intensity. For example, a student may believe strongly in conservation of natural resources and demonstrate his belief as he talks to others, writes letters to legislators, and works toward conservation goals. Conversely, the same student may say that he believes in organized religion, but neither talk nor work toward church goals.

To judge a person's attitudes and beliefs on the basis of self-reports may be misleading. Observation of behavior is a better means of determining attitudes and beliefs, as long as the observer observes and reports the exact behavior and does not attempt to analyze its significance. Only one who prepares case studies concerning beliefs and attitudes of an individual can interpret an individual's complex, ambiguous beliefs and attitudes.

PRACTITIONERS *(Inter-differences)   Students come to school with all types of attitudes and beliefs about themselves, society, and institutions. They have different religions and political and social beliefs, and their attitudes toward any one thing will vary considerably.*

Students have reputations for having either good or poor attitudes, according to the teacher's own internalized beliefs about appropriate classroom behavior. If students have the attitudes and beliefs of the social middle class, they are generally identified as possessing good attitudes. If their attitudes and beliefs deviate from the middle-class norm, they are labeled as having poor attitudes. A certain amount of deviation from middle-class attitudes and be-

liefs may be tolerated in certain situations, depending on the individual student and school and community mores.

Depending on family background and other environmental influences, each student develops a set of attitudes and beliefs that are uniquely his own, and applies them to the society in which he lives.

THEORISTS *(Inter-differences) Students' attitudes are affected by the beliefs and attitudes of family and friends; by the educational system they attend; by textbooks, television, movies, magazines and newspapers; and by church, social, and institutional groups. In each instance, the individual experiences and interacts with a unique pattern of influences that causes him to incorporate these beliefs and attitudes into a system that is highly individualistic.*

The public schools influence the beliefs and attitudes of students to a large extent. Many students are influenced by the personal attitudes of popular teachers. Perhaps teacher-training institutions and public school personnel directors should be more selective in regard to teachers' beliefs and attitudes, considering how they may affect students in the public schools.

After a full morning's work, practitioners and theorists join forces to discuss the implications that individual differences have for education. Following is a transcript of the session.

EDUCATIONAL IMPLICATIONS

CHAIRMAN *This meeting has been arranged for the purpose of sharing today's ideas and discussing any implications they have for teachers. During the summation, I hope we can participate in an open discussion concerning all the issues involved.*

PRACTITIONER NO. 1 *The fact that students are different was evident to me before I arrived this morning, but today I became more aware that students differ in so many ways.*

THEORIST NO. 1 *Yes, it seems evident to me that even if instructor and student were paired on a one-to-one basis, it would be impossible for the instructor to meet all the individual needs of that one student.*

PRACTITIONER NO. 2 *Maybe individualized instruction is a goal for teachers rather than a reality. We have other instances of goals in American society, such as striving for a true democracy, or the individual striving to live a Christian life. Are these individual goals somewhat similar to individualized instructional goals in education?*

THEORIST NO. 2 *I would agree that individuals differ in so many ways that one teacher in a classroom teaching thirty students is capable of individualizing only to the degree that the situation allows. The classroom teaching situation that bothers me, however, is one in which a mechanized teacher teaches only grade-level materials to all students without regard to students' abilities.*

PRACTITIONER NO. 3 *When we talk about classroom teaching situations, we must remember that teachers do not always have a free hand for individualizing instruction. Teachers are constrained by grade-standards theorists who contend that all students in a certain grade should study subject matter on the same level. Some administrators even insist that all students study material from the same textbook page.*

PRACTITIONER NO. 4 *While we are talking about constraints, we might as well mention other situations that often hinder individualized instructional efforts. Teachers may face overcrowded classes, crowded teaching space, antiquated furniture, scarcity of resources and materials, and faculty peers who want to mass-teach from materials prepared for them.*

THEORIST NO. 3 *I would agree that some situations make individualized instruction more difficult, yet, we find instances where teachers in negative situations are individualizing. In other instances, teachers placed in wonderful situations for individualizing refuse to let their surroundings influence their traditional philosophies and practices. I do not have any research data to verify this statement, but I believe individualized instructional practices in any particular classroom are more teacher-oriented than situation-oriented.*

PRACTITIONER NO. 5 *May I change the subject just a little? As I attend this conference, one thing preys on my mind. If we intend to attempt to meet the needs of students in our classes, shouldn't we consider not only how our students differ, but also how they are alike? It seems to me that if we develop programs and strategies merely on the basis of differences, then we are not taking advantage of our knowledge of ways in which students are alike. Classroom activities that have each student learning something differ-*

ent prevent them from interacting, learning from each other, and developing their interpersonal relationship skills.

THEORIST NO. 4   *Comprehensive individualized instructional programs that incorporate broad goals and objectives and take into consideration both student differences and likenesses have a better chance for acceptance from everyone concerned. Programs built solely on computer or machine teaching, independent study techniques, ability grouping, or any other narrow definition of individualized instruction will have to overcome their restricted scope limitations if they are to become permanent programs.*

THEORIST NO. 2   *I disagree with my colleague. I believe some of the programs he mentions are viable programs that will become permanent fixtures for education in America.*

PRACTITIONER NO. 6   *During the past twenty-five years, the individualized educational movement, with its many definitions and variety of programs, has certainly become a valid movement in American education. Yet, there is still more talk than action. Why?*

PRACTITIONER NO. 2   *Because it is popular to talk about individualized instruction. Educators are prone to talk about it on one hand and operate on a different basis when they return to their school situations. I believe that we accept those things with which we can agree, and we are likely to reject programs and activities that do not meet our individual teaching needs or philosophies.*

THEORIST NO. 6   *Also, talking about individualized instruction is much easier than actually practicing what one preaches.*

PRACTITIONER NO. 6   *If professors in colleges of education would practice what they preach, and make their classes models of individualized instruction, the gap between talking about individualized instruction and practicing it would become a small one.*

THEORIST NO. 6   *I agree with that statement! In defense of teacher education, I would like to say that movement in the direction of your concerns is being made.*

PRACTITIONER NO. 5   *I believe teacher education is the responsibility of all arms of the profession—colleges of education, the public schools, and professional groups. One arm of the profession blames another for the inadequacies and failures of teacher education. I believe the time has come for all of us to work together as an organized team to improve professionally.*

PRACTITIONER NO. 1 *One other constraint that is always mentioned when teachers talk about individualized instruction is the grades and grading obstacle. Most school systems still adhere to traditional grading practices that require teachers to compare students in their classrooms. Individualized instruction and comparative grading systems do not correspond.*

THEORIST NO. 3 *During the past two decades, a modification of traditional grading policies has developed into a trend. Still, an ambivalent situation exists in a majority of school situations. When instructional philosophies and evaluative philosophies do not jibe, students, teachers, and parents are confused.*

PRACTITIONER NO. 2 *I prefer not to spend time debating the grades and grading issue! I would like to state that I prefer a teaching situation that does not force me into a predetermined model of individualized instruction or evaluation. I have a broad concept concerning individualized instruction, and I want enough freedom to operate in my classroom on the basis of my beliefs.*

PRACTITIONER NO. 6 *I agree with you; however, I do think that all of us should be open to new programs and instructional strategies. A closed mind may lead one to become static and stale in his teaching-learning situation.*

CHAIRMAN *It seems to me that our statements signify that each of us is different! We project points of view from our own frame of reference. Sometimes we agree, and at other times we disagree. To attend a meeting like this for the purpose of noting the differences that exist among participants is a worthwhile experience. I hope that this meeting will serve as a prelude to significant professional development activities for everyone. The meeting is adjourned.*

SUGGESTED READINGS

ANASTASI, ANNE. *Differential Psychology.* 3rd ed. New York: Macmillan Co., 1958.

ANASTASI, ANNE. *Individual Differences.* New York: John Wiley & Sons, 1965.

BLOOM, BENJAMIN S. *Stability and Change in Human Characteristics.* New York: John Wiley & Sons, 1964.

DECECCO, JOHN P. *Psychology of Learning and Instruction.* Englewood Cliffs, N.J.: Prentice-Hall, 1968.

ESTVAN, FRANK J. *Social Studies in a Changing World.* New York: Harcourt, Brace & World, 1968.

JAROLIMEK, JOHN. *Social Studies in the Elementary School.* New York: Macmillan Co., 1971.

TYLER, LEONA E. *Individual Differences: Abilities and Motivational Directions.* New York: Appleton-Century-Crofts, 1973.

VI. Accountability in Individualized Student Evaluation

Reporting Individualized Evaluation Results to
Students and Parents
Philosophy and Practice

A written philosophy of evaluation should be formulated by individual schools, based on the combined thinking of the faculty. Philosophies are based on individual attitudes and beliefs; however, teachers may find these tenets—the foundations of American democracy—useful in arriving at a philosophy of educational evaluation.

1. The public schools have an important function to perform so that America may remain a free, democratic society. Evaluative practices should help develop a feeling of "we-ness" in at least a majority of students. In other words, the practices should promote a feeling that all students are worthy and belong in the public school.

2. Student appraisal should support the most fundamental tenet of democracy: a concern for the individual and a desire to permit and foster the development of the individual. A curriculum should be designed for the individual within the framework of school objectives, and evaluation should be concerned with the individual's growth and development in relation to his ability and effort.

3. Educators have a responsibility for the development and evaluation of important learning outcomes in the areas of the intellectual, physical, emotional, and social spheres of the human personality. The intellectual domain cannot be placed in a compartment and measured in isolation. Assessment procedures should measure all areas of the individual, because the areas are interdependent.

4. Ever since the first tax-supported schools were established, the ideal that public school education should be for *ALL* American children has been nurtured as a paramount concern of the American people. As a result, a literate electorate has made the democratic form of government possible. It seems evident that if all American children must attend the public schools, then each student should have the right to equal educational opportunity.

5. An essential part of evaluation is student self-evaluation. Involving students in a cooperative self-evaluative enter-

prise to recognize goals and objectives in relation to their own abilities and weaknesses motivates students to attain these goals and to experience success.

6. Every child is unique, and each individual is precious. The predominant relationship role for the teacher is to be a helper, and all evaluative procedures should be judged on the basis of helping the student to become.

A great deal of emphasis has been placed on individualized instruction in recent years. Teachers are asked to measure student achievement levels in subject matter areas and to prescribe learning experiences for individual students. As a student progresses through learning experiences designed specifically for him, the teacher helps him to reach his goals and provides positive reinforcement for him as he attains these goals according to his own abilities. But then the effectiveness of the instructional procedure is blunted when teachers are forced to play the grading game.

Beliefs about student evaluation are based on one's philosophy of education. Teachers attempt to reconcile their personal beliefs about student evaluation to the grading practices of a particular school system. So they must subjectively adjust their grading estimate according to their particular philosophy. While one teacher may place major emphasis on individual capabilities and attainments when measuring students' academic accomplishments, another teacher may regard age and grade comparisons as the predominant criteria emphasis. In both instances, the particular teacher is forced to compromise his beliefs in order to accommodate the system.

Teachers are confused as they face the dilemma of placing grades on just about everything a student does at school. Teachers try to grade tests, themes, written exercises, scrapbooks, workbooks, assignments, projects, class participation, oral reports, and numerous other activities. Teachers are asked to measure each student's academic accomplishments in terms of his individual capabilities and attainments, as well as to compare his achievement with that of other students of comparable age and grade level. They are expected to use only one symbol to designate how well the student is achieving individually and how well he is doing in comparison to others. That is impossible. It is the same as placing a chicken and a fox in the same cage and asking them to live together. Individualized instruction and comparative grading cannot exist in harmony with each other.

Most school systems have developed goals and objectives in every subject. These goals and objectives are usually written for students according to age and grade level. Textbooks, curriculum guides, independent study packets, instructional modules, and daily lesson plans help teachers to determine the scope of the subject matter and to break it down into teachable segments for daily instruction. It is crucial to realize, however, that students do not achieve according to age and grade level norms. Each student progresses toward academic goals and objectives according to an individualized rate and time frame. Goals and objectives should not be scuttled, but neither should they become barriers for students who cannot reach them, or for those who may be able to achieve far beyond the goals and objectives for their age and grade level. Individualized evaluative procedures would require teachers to keep files of students' work samples consistently. Students' work samples and progress record files should be kept as meticulously as a bookkeeper keeps business records. Individualized student-centric teaching techniques yield a wealth of data for the perceptive teacher, and on the basis of daily work samples, the teacher can check the progress of a student in relation to goals and objectives. Either the student has demonstrated competency regarding certain knowledge or skill, or he has not. If he has demonstrated competency, records and work samples will indicate what the student has accomplished. If he has not demonstrated competency, records and work samples will reveal the student's inadequacies, and then records should be kept listing the remedial and recycling procedures necessary for the individual.

An essential part of individualized evaluation in the modern school is self-evaluation. Students are motivated to improve when they help set individual goals. As they reach these goals, they experience satisfaction because they recognize that progress has been made. Results should be reviewed by teachers and students so that together they realize evidence of progress; then, strengths and weaknesses may be noted so that students, with teacher support, may diagnose their difficulties and be ready for the next learning experience. Some teachers spend so much time grading papers that they do not have sufficient time to teach or to evaluate students. Student papers that teachers mark in red to point out student errors and return long after the learning activities occur do not serve as effective learning experiences for students. Evaluation should be a process that is accomplished *with* students on a daily basis. Instead, in many instances, evaluation is a strange and mysterious phenomenon that happens *to* students at the end of sacrosanct grading periods.

Individualized evaluation, as described in the previous paragraphs, may be defined as evaluation of an individual student's attainment and progress in relation to his own starting point while both student and teacher strive to reach and surpass goals and objectives that have been set for particular age groups or grade levels. To attempt to persuade people that individualized evaluation is this simple is a formidable task, because they cannot separate student evaluation practices from reporting methods.

REPORTING INDIVIDUALIZED EVALUATION RESULTS TO STUDENTS AND PARENTS

Reports to parents about their children are based on information that results from the evaluation of students, but preparing reporting forms and initiating procedures that relay information to parents about their children's progress in school are beset with complexities. Their importance requires that any information conveyed must be positive, clear, and complete with specific details.

Whether a particular school system uses reporting forms, parent-teacher conferences, or a combination of the two procedures, reporting on an individual basis should be the responsibility of teachers. Goals and objectives should be stated in behavioral terms. Then learning segment competencies that result in the attainment of goals and objectives for subject matter areas must be listed in sequence in learner terminology. Using a bar graph, the teacher can show the progress a student has made in relation to the goals and objectives set forth. If the learning segments are too numerous, usually they can be combined, edited, or stated in broad terms, so that parents will have time to see the picture without being immersed in an avalanche of irrelevant data. Figure 6.1 is a sample of an individualized reporting form.

An individualized reporting form has certain strengths and advantages over traditional reporting forms:

1. Both students and teachers are held accountable for learning.
2. The teacher reports achievement in concrete terms

NAME: _Jane Doe_   TEACHER: _Miss Pringle_

SCHOOL: _Woodville School_   COUNSELOR: _Mr. Bean_

Progress Rate	Key	Student's Achievement Level at _equiv-_ Close of School Term _8.6 Grade alent_

		Number of segments depends on Individual Student
blue	BLUE AREA shows progress for SIXTH REPORTING PERIOD	Instructional Segment Behavioral Components #12
		Instructional Segment Behavioral Components #11
yellow	YELLOW AREA shows progress for FIFTH REPORTING PERIOD	Instructional Segment Behavioral Components #10
		Instructional Segment Behavioral Components # 9
black	BLACK AREA shows progress for FOURTH REPORTING PERIOD	Instructional Segment Behavioral Components # 8
		Instructional Segment Behavioral Components # 7
green	GREEN AREA shows progress for THIRD REPORTING PERIOD	Instructional Segment Behavioral Components # 6
		Instructional Segment Behavioral Components # 5
brown	BROWN AREA shows progress for SECOND REPORTING PERIOD	Instructional Segment Behavioral Components # 4
		Instructional Segment Behavioral Components # 3
red	RED AREA shows progress for FIRST REPORTING PERIOD	Instructional Segment Behavioral Components # 2
		Instructional Segment Behavioral Components # 1

Content Area
Math

Student's Achievement Level at Beginning of School Term
7.1 Grade Equivalent

FIGURE 6.1 Individualized Reporting Form

rather than making value judgments based on subjective data.

3. Teachers evaluate students in terms of their own abilities and are not forced to compare students with others.
4. Individualized reporting forms activate individualized instructional strategies and procedures.
5. Teachers are not forced to play the grading game with students and parents.

Teachers can prepare an individualized report form for each subject. The goals and objectives for each of the subjects should be placed in an attractive brochure, which should also contain explanations of the reporting philosophy and procedures.

Teachers should also have the responsibility for reporting to parents about the social and emotional development of individual students, but again, these reports should not be value-judgment reports. Sociometric devices may be used to evaluate student growth in social relations. Observational techniques that use behavior problem categories, charts, and anecdotal records help teachers to evaluate emotional and social development. Experience summaries, diaries, and logs are particularly useful for making valid statements about a student's social and emotional growth. Parents should receive information concerning the student's study and work habits so that they can understand his progress in relation to his effort. This format is currently used on most communications to parents; however, to be valuable the items must be stated in positive terms using precise language so that parents may receive specific, relevant data. The Personal Growth Form in Figure 6.2 contains samples of well-written items.

Reports to parents should indicate their child's individual attainment and progress in relation to his individual ability and effort. However, parents also need to know how well their child is achieving in comparison with others so that they can help plan his educational and vocational future. Results of standardized tests furnish comparative information using a percentile profile chart. Standardized tests should be developed locally by competent personnel, and comparative data should be sent to parents from the *counselor's* or *principal's* office. Comparative data reporting forms should relay comparative information to parents using a meaningful, understandable reporting format. Percentiles, quartiles, and mean points on charts may be confusing even though explanations are thorough, so a simplified reporting form such as the one in Figure 6.3 can be constructed.

EMOTIONAL GROWTH: *Check the following items if the student is observed practicing the behavior often enough to be a behavior pattern*

NAME: _____

Sample Items:

1. Practices Self-Control
- ✓ a. Able to control temper
- ✓ b. Able to recover quickly when disappointed
- ✓ c. Able to concentrate for reasonable periods of time
- ✓ d. Able to listen as much as he talks
- ✓ e. Willing to participate
- ✓ f. Able to resolve personal disputes without fighting
- ✓ g. Practices good manners
- ✓ h. Is considerate of feelings of others
- ✓ i. Is wide awake and eager to learn
- ✓ j. Is willing to share "star" status with others
- ✓ k. Is free of annoying mannerisms
- ✓ l. Practices discretion concerning appropriate times for using restroom and drinking fountain facilities

2. Accepts Responsibilities
- ✓ a. Keeps class and school rules
- ✓ b. Finishes assigned tasks
- ✓ c. Is on time to appointed places
- ✓ d. Practices good sportsmanship
- ✓ e. Respects property rights
- ✓ f. Participates in planning activities

3. Study and Work Habits
- ✓ a. Works accurately and neatly
- ✓ b. Works well alone
- ✓ c. Practices good study habits
- ✓ d. Contributes to class activities

STUDENT: _____*Jane Doe*_____

Social Growth

Sample Items:

_____ Students choosing _*Jane*_ as one they wanted to work with preparing class work projects _7_

_____ Classmates choosing _*Jane*_ as one they wanted as a partner for play activities _10_

_____ Classmates _*Jane*_ reports he likes _20_

_____ Classmates reporting _*Jane*_ likes them _25_

_____ Prefers to spend time with:
- a. all class members _a_
- b. a selected group
- c. close personal friend
- d. alone

_____ Fulfills the following roles in group situations:
- a. leader ✓
- b. talker ✓
- c. initiator ✓
- d. evaluator _____
- e. arbitrator _____
- f. summarizer _____
- g. independent thinker ✓
- h. questioner ✓

FIGURE 6.2 Personal Growth Form

NAME: _____

Checked items are evidenced often enough to be considered important by the teacher

I. Vision:
- ____ a. Strains to read chalkboard
- ____ b. Holds book very close to eyes
- ____ c. Holds book on one side
- ____ d. Has frequent eye infections

Nurse's Report:

II. Hearing:
- ____ a. Often fails to respond to a spoken request
- ____ b. Cups ear with hand
- ____ c. Turns head to one side when listening
- ____ d. Has frequent earaches and infections

Nurse's Report:

III. Speech:
- ____ a. Has articulation problems
- ____ b. Omits or substitutes sounds
- ____ c. Lisping is a problem
- ____ d. Difficult to understand

Nurse's Report:

IV. Dental:
- ✓ a. Practices positive dental hygiene
- ✓ b. Needs to consider corrective braces
- ____ c. Cavities in evidence

Nurse's Report:

V. Nutrition:
- ____ a. Has energy loss in mid-morning or mid-afternoon because of food intake
- ____ b. Over or underweight for age, height, and bone structure
- ✓ c. School diet not nutritionally balanced
- ✓ d. Does not drink enough water
- ____ e. Over uses sugar or salt

Nurse's Report on Health Practice Inventory

VI. Absence Due to Illness:
- ____ a. Has frequent colds
- ____ b. Listless or apathetic
- ____ c. Has frequent infections
- ____ d. Seems sleepy or tired
- ____ e. Confirmed mouth breather
- ____ f. Physical activity causes shortness of breath
- ____ g. Shows sudden weight loss
- ____ h. Exhibits signs of being hyperactive
- ____ i. Stumbles or falls often
- ____ j. Bruises easily
- ____ k. Other health problems in evidence

Nurse's Report:

VII. Physical Activities:

Physical Fitness Scores: *passed tests on following*
- ✓ 1. Running
- ✓ 2. Jumping
- ____ 3. Chinning
- ____ 4. Rope Skipping

Playground Activities

Participation List: (Example: Sample List for One Student)
- ____ 1. Tennis
- ____ 2. Table Tennis
- ____ 3. Softball
- ____ 4. Swimming
- ____ 5. Tumbling
- ____ 6. Volley Ball
- ____ 7. Track Events
- ____ 8. Student's Choice
- ____ 9. Lifted Weights

FIGURE 6.2 (CONT)

NAME: _____ TEST: _____

SCHOOL: _____ COUNSELOR: _____

Percentage of students of same age and grade level who rank above your student on this particular test is
ABOVE THE HEAVY LINE

Percentage of students of same age and grade level who rank below your student on this particular test is
BELOW THE HEAVY\LINE

THE HEAVY LINE REPRESENTS YOUR STUDENT'S
PERCENTILE RANK

Each *Heavy* Line Represents FIVE PERCENTILE POINTS						
SUBJECT	SUBJECT	SUBJECT	SUBJECT	SUBJECT	SUBJECT	SUBJECT
					19% above	
25% above					80% below	
74% below		29% above				
		70% below				
				39% above		
				60% below		
						55% above
	59% above					44% below
	40% below					
			69% above			
			30% below			

FIGURE 6.3 Comparative Data Report Form

As a public school proposes change in the way students are to be evaluated—especially changes in reporting instruments—parents, students, school personnel, and other segments of the community should be involved in developing and implementing the proposed change. Public meetings that offer parents opportunities to learn and to discuss the merits of individualized evaluation are essential. Brochures that explain the reporting philosophy, procedures, and forms become a part of the reporting materials, and school conferences with teachers, parents, counselors, and principals help to bridge the gap between the traditional and the newly created process.

Identical instruction for all students and evaluation based on comparison must be replaced by a differentiated education, which allows differences in the levels of achievement expected by students. If the public schools profess a belief in individualizing instruction, as a corollary they must be willing to accept individualized evaluation as a necessary part of the total process.

PHILOSOPHY AND PRACTICE

Although individualized instruction in its many forms has gained acceptance, student evaluation based on individual attainment according to ability and effort is not a common practice. A large majority of the school systems retain a marking system whereby a grade is used to connote a student's performance in a subject. Numerals, letters, and other symbols are used to record data on permanent records and to report to students, parents, and others information concerning the student's level of performance in those things that the school evaluates. Usually, the same symbol is used to designate the student's individual attainment according to ability and effort and to designate his achievement in relation to other students of comparable age and grade. The teacher's personal philosophy of education becomes the bulwark for his evaluative practice when he is faced with this incongruent situation.

At one end of the philosophical continuum are grade-standard theorists who believe in comparative grading and strict adherence to grade standards as requirements for promotion. Equal-educational-opportunity theorists are at the opposite end of the continuum. They believe that the public schools should be dedicated to serving the educational needs of students as individuals, and that teachers should be asked only to measure student achievement on the basis of individual capabilities and attainments. Few teachers are puristic grade-standard theorists or equal-opportunity theorists. A vast majority would espouse an evaluative philosophy resting between these polar positions. Regardless of what they say they believe, however, their true philosophy is put into practice when they instruct and evaluate students.

Two common examples of teacher behavior—one on the secondary school level and one at the elementary school level—illustrate the grades and grading dilemma teachers face, and how they actually practice what their philosophies dictate.

The secondary school scene takes place in the faculty lounge, where two English teachers who teach the same English composition section for high school seniors are drinking their morning cup of coffee. There is no sound in the lounge except the sounds of two people sipping hot coffee. Martha, fiftyish, looks like the conservative type. She raises her head and peers over half-glasses at Linda.

"Linda, don't you have Peggy Williams in your class this year?" Martha knows that Peggy is in Linda's third-period class, but this is Martha's tenth year at Marvel High School and her twenty-fifth year of teaching English, and Linda is in her third year of teaching. Martha wishes to sound her out concerning her grading philosophy. "You know that Peggy failed my class last year?"

"Yes, I know that this is Peggy's second time around." Linda's voice matches the calm assurance she feels as a young teacher of firm convictions. "She is attending class and working up to her capability, however."

Martha tries another sip of coffee, and the bitter taste causes her to purse her lips as she ponders her next words. "Linda, you do recognize that we have very high standards at Marvel High. Our records show that 93 percent of our graduates attend college, and it will be a disgrace to all graduates if Peggy receives a diploma."

"Martha, I do not believe that all the seniors receiving diplomas last year were college prospects."

"Well, Linda, you know that Peggy just does not have the ability to write a theme. Her sentence structure is atrocious." Martha's tone emphasizes that her assessment of the student is unquestionable as well as final.

Linda's brown eyes sparkle with warm enthusiasm as she leans forward in her chair. "I know. That's why she has been expanding sentences and working on structure by filling in slots with correct words. She's making real progress."

The sincerity in her tone is lost on Martha who is thinking of the work she has done preparing a curriculum guide for teachers to follow in teaching the course Peggy is repeating. Her feelings cause her to stand looking down at Linda.

"Linda, I believe in helping students who are having difficulties with the requirements of the course, but a student must learn English grammar, and all the exercises necessary must be taught. I spend many hours outside class time helping students, but I do feel that all students should fulfill the same requirements for credit in this course."

Linda recognizes the pending confrontation. She realizes that Martha has attained faculty status and community power, and she decides to evade the issue. She changes the subject, but vows to herself that she will follow her own integrity and put her philosophy into practice. If Peggy continues her present performance, she will pass English this time!

The elementary school scene begins with Dan Marsh sitting at his desk. He is trying to decide on Buddy Shirley's math grade for the current six-week period. A letter symbol must be recorded on Buddy's permanent record, and the same grade will be placed on a reporting form to be sent home to his parents. As the teacher computes daily marks, he notes that he has grades recorded for assignments, homework, workbook pages, tests, class participation, and daily written exercises.

Dan Marsh is faced with a dilemma each time he computes an average for a student, but he is confronted with a special problem in Buddy's case. The teacher pauses to ponder the situation. Buddy has made good grades when he has been placed in subject matter at his own level, but he ranks in the lower quarter of the class when he is compared to classmates.

For recording and reporting Buddy's progress, Dan is using three measuring categories to compute grades. Table 6.1 helps him to examine his philosophy of education in terms of his grading practices.

Dan believes in individualized instruction, but reporting practices require him to record Buddy's grade on a permanent record with a letter grade that encompasses how well he achieves in relation to his ability and how well he achieves when compared to other students. This grade will be placed on a report card and extended to Buddy, his parents, and friends.

The teacher has helped Buddy to achieve at his own

TABLE 6.1

BUDDY SHIRLEY — MATH

I. *Progress Made in Relation to Ability a effort*

Stanford Benet Group Test	=	IQ 100
SRA Achievement Series	=	One grade below level
Individualized Instructional Segments Completed Written Exercises	=	25
Workbook Exercises on Student Level	=	All Completed

PROGRESS MADE

Instructional Segments Test Average	=	90% Correct
Comparative Achievement Tests Progress	=	10 Percentile Points

EFFORT: Works in Class and Completes Homework Assignments

II. *Achievement Compared with Others in Class*

Teacher-Made Achievement Tests	=	Ranked 15th in Class of 25
Standardized Achievement Test	=	Ranked 16th in Class of 25

III. *Achievement Compared to Age-and Grade-Level Expectations and National Norms*

Grade-Level Objectives Completed	=	One grade below level
Educational Age	=	10 months below chronological age
Standardized Test Percentile Score	=	35th Percentile

---

level, and he has told him many times that he is doing well. A low grade for Buddy might be detrimental to their interpersonal relationship, and the low grade might lower Buddy's feelings of self-esteem, which have been on the rise lately. At the same time, the teacher knows that the school principal and Buddy's parents will misunderstand a high grade in math, and the teacher who will teach Buddy the next year might not understand how Buddy had achieved so well in math in Dan's class when his achievement level is almost a year below grade-level norms.

Dan Marsh must consider his personal philosophy of grades and grading in relation to local school grading and reporting practices. He really believes that the student should receive an *A* yet feels that an *A* will not be acceptable to the school system or to the parents in the community. A compromise is in order, but the teacher's compromise permits him to maintain a clear conscience. The teacher records a *B* for Buddy's six-week math grade.

In a special meeting called for the purpose of investigating grading practices, Mr. Marsh presents the chart he has used and asks Martha and Linda to place an emphasis percentage estimate in each of the measuring categories. Emphasis percentage estimates are collected, and the results are depicted in Table 6.2. The chart did not instigate an argument among these teachers. The results helped them to understand the basis for a part of the grading dilemma that faces all teachers. Just as the general public has diverse opinions concerning grades and grading, teachers have different beliefs also.

TABLE 6.2

	Martha	*Linda*	*Dan*
Percentage of grade based on progress made in relation to ability and effort	10%	60%	80%
Percentage of grade based on achievement compared with other students in class	30%	15%	5%
Percentage of grade based on age- and grade-level expectations and national norms	60%	25%	15%

The purpose of including philosophy and practice as a part of individualized evaluation is to emphasize the following points:

Whether a person believes in individualized evaluation or evaluation based on comparison with others depends on his philosophy of education.

If a teacher is employed in a school with a traditional grading system, and he believes in individualized instruction, his basis for evaluation will favor individual progress made in relation to ability and effort.

If a teacher is employed in a school with a traditional grading
system, and he believes in grade and age-level standards,
he will favor teaching subject matter on an achievement
level for that particular grade. The major emphasis for
determining grades is placed on the comparison of the .
individual student with others.

If a teacher is employed in a school system with a grading
philosophy that is in accord with his instructional and
evaluative philosophies, he is a fortunate individual.

SUGGESTED READINGS

BEGGS, DAVID W., and BUFFE, EDWARD G. *Non-graded
Schools in Action.* Bloomington: Indiana University
Press, 1967.

BLOOM, BENJAMIN S. *Handbook: Formative and Summative
Evaluation of Learning.* New York: McGraw-Hill, 1971.

GLASSER, WILLIAM. *Schools without Failure.* New York:
Harper & Row, Publishers, 1969.

LESSINGER, LEON. *Every Kid a Winner.* New York: Simon &
Schuster, 1970.

LEWKSBURY, JOHN L. *Non-grading in the Elementary School.*
Columbus, O.: Charles E. Merrill Books, 1967.

MUSGRAVE, G. RAY. *The Grading Game: A Public School
Fiasco.* New York: Vantage Press, 1970.

OTTO, HENRY J., and SANDERS, DAVID C. *Elementary School
Organization and Administration. 4th ed.* New York:
Appleton-Century-Crofts, 1964.

SAWIN, ENOCH. *Evaluation and The work of the Teacher.*
Belmont, Calif.: Wadsworth Publishing Co., 1969.

VII. *Implementing Programs that Focus on the Learner*

Organization Plans
Operational Format for Focus-on-the-Learner
    Projects
Program Content (Phase One)
Program Content (Phase Two)
Summer Work Sessions
Pre-Semester Workshops
Competency-Based Teacher Education as a
    Vehicle for Implementing Focus-on-the-
    Learner Strategies
Program Evaluation

If preservice and in-service programs designed to take place in the public schools are to reach a state of excellence, all concerned parties must agree to certain underlying conditions:

1. Teacher education and training is a responsibility of all arms of the teaching profession, including colleges of education, public school systems, and the organized profession. For years, all parties have voiced a spirit of cooperation, but each group has refused to share what it believes are its autonomous rights. Public school systems benevolently allow colleges of education to send preservice teachers into their schools, and college professors strive mightily through theory courses to remold preservice and in-service teachers, but both parties renege when asked to work towards common goals or to amalgamate finances or teaching staffs. Meanwhile, the staff members of professional organizations plan meetings to improve teacher education, but the organized profession has been unable to lessen differences or to become partners in teacher-education programs.

   In the future, preparing teachers initially and educating teachers in-service should be done in training cadres by people from colleges of education, the public schools, and the professional agencies. Such a concept implies the acceptance of a differentiated staff, the use of talent from each strata of the education profession, and a new emphasis on interrelationships between professional personnel in teacher-training institutions and in the public schools. A team approach is necessary, or else the chasm that exists between theory and practice will remain as absolute as ever, and education will continue to be locked into the status quo.

2. Teacher-training programs must be competency-based. They must first provide teachers in training with knowledge, rather than just theory, and then require them to perform competently in teaching-learning situations with students in the public schools. Field training must be part of the program so that teacher trainers can actually

144

demonstrate those practices that they merely talked about in the past and preservice students and in-service teachers can participate in a situation where theory and practice merge to become a teaching-learning reality.

In order for such a program to be successful, all people involved must agree that its goal is to produce teachers who will be competent when they operate in actual classroom settings. Everyone must also agree that program participants must be allowed to grow toward self-actualization while they are teaching.

3. An educational program is deficient if there is no way to evaluate its effectiveness or the effectiveness of its product. More emphasis should be placed on measuring and evaluating programs in relation to short-term and long-range product effectiveness. If generic and specific competencies have been listed for either preservice or in-service programs, then, of course, participants should be measured as being competent or proficient as they demonstrate each particular competency. Total effectiveness, though, can only be measured at the termination point, and lasting effectiveness can be measured through the use of carefully designed follow-up evaluative procedures. When the people responsible for educating and training teachers are held accountable for the effectiveness of those teachers in the program, the focus will be placed where it belongs: *on the needs and accomplishments of the learner.*

4. Although most professional educators agree that preservice and in-service programs of the past have been to a large degree ineffective, the assumption that any group will readily agree to a different approach is erroneous. However, any program that does not provide the participants with cognitive input and experiences that help them to conceptualize and believe in the philosophy and goals of the program is doomed to failure.

Participant readiness programs should be conducted by leaders who are effective change agents; i.e., the leaders should possess clear perceptions concerning the proposed programs, and their interpersonal relations and practices should exemplify the proposed change. Effective leaders will recognize the need to involve participants in sessions and experiences to clarify concepts before actually attempting to implement the program. Participant readiness is an essential underlying condition that must be accomplished before any program can be successful.

5. Although federal funds have provided revenue for many successful pilot programs, financial support for planning

and implementing effective programs must be provided from a more stabilized source. The same source that provides funds for other essential components of the educational system should provide money for research projects, otherwise educators will continue to write proposals for new programs that cannot be put into effect because they have no financial support.

Financial support for curriculum and instructional excellence must be provided so that effective professional development programs can be implemented on a long-term basis and thus become an integral part of the total program. A total commitment to the financial support of worthwhile programs on a continuing basis is an underlying condition to their success.

Of course, professional development programs need not be postponed until these underlying conditions are resolved. Professional development programs continue to improve in spite of obstacles, but the professional development situation is critical enough for all concerned to attempt to provide underlying conditions that will result in more effective programs.

ORGANIZATION PLANS

The following organizational plans are described only because pilot programs have been completed. Application of each plan was dependent on the purposes and needs of a particular school system. Other plans and ideas for implementing in-depth field-service programs may be more worthy when applied to other locations or personnel. If a field-service program is to be effective, however, an organizational structure that provides teachers with in-depth experiences must be provided.

In-Service Center Plan

During the school year 1970–71, an in-service center plan was piloted in the northeast area of the Houston Independent School District. The federally funded project established a professional development center at Ryan Elementary School to train primary teachers from eight elementary schools that were close together in the heart of the low-income area of the district. Ryan Elementary School is a typical school of the area; however, Title I funds were provided by the state to build a modern in-service building in the center of the campus.

The organizational plan called for five university consultants, five district staff personnel, eight elementary school principals, eight master teachers (one for each primary class attending Ryan School), sixteen replacement teachers who rotated from school to school, and the ninety-six satellite teachers who were trainees in the program. (Figure 7.1 is an organization schema of a central in-service plan.) The period of participation for each group of trainee teachers was fixed at six weeks, with five days set aside for transition requirements. Two satellite teachers from each school go to Ryan Center each six weeks. Revolving teachers replace them in their classrooms.

The in-service center plan placed two satellite teachers with each master teacher in a regular classroom situation. The master teacher demonstrated strategies that the satellite teachers had previously learned about in laboratory sessions with consultants. After a critique and discussion session, each satellite teacher performed the same procedures. All three teachers worked together in the regular classroom from 8:45 to 11:30 in the morning. After lunch, satellite teachers met for an hour each day with consultants while the master teachers remained in the regular classroom. Satellite teachers, master teachers, and consultants met on Friday afternoons to prepare materials, to evaluate experiences, to participate in group and individual conferences, and at times to engage in question and answer sessions.

The real strengths of an in-service center plan include the following:

1. Teachers receive an in-depth experience using focus-on-the-learner methods in a regular classroom.
2. Teachers are placed with other teachers who are adept at teaching and working with others effectively in a regular classroom with all types of students.
3. Teachers not only observe other teachers using a variety of techniques and methods, but they are allowed to practice the methods and observe themselves, using videotape playbacks of their lessons.
4. A stimulating, enthusiastic atmosphere causes groups of teachers to return to their regular classes with renewed vigor and a more wholesome outlook.

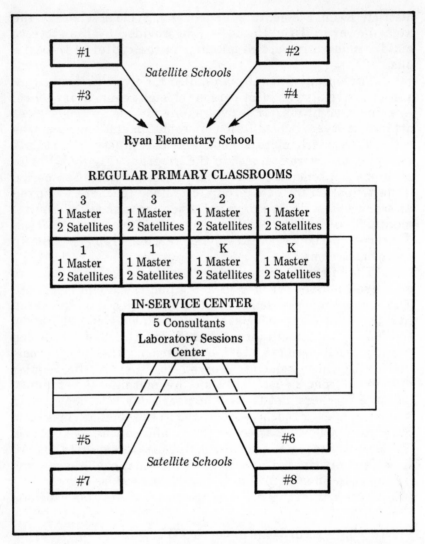

FIGURE 7.1 Organizational Schema For Central In-Service Plan

The primary weakness is financial. The center itself is not so costly, but the salaries of the sixteen replacement teachers, who are actually extra teachers, constitute a large expenditure. Satellite principals must receive in-depth experience in the focus-on-the-learner concepts and really believe in the methodology so that strong, effective follow-up programs will be in effect when the satellite teacher returns from the in-service center to his regular assignment. Otherwise, the service-center experience for the teacher will just be a period of interruption from old methods and practices, which they will soon be influenced to adopt once again.

Mobile-Unit Plan

During the school years 1971–72 and 1972–73, a mobile-unit plan entitled the Teaching Strategies Program operated district-wide in the Houston Independent School District. The Teaching Strategies Program employed a director and twenty-four teaching specialists to work full time in the elementary schools. Trained specialists worked in teams of four, rotating from school to school at designated time intervals. Each Friday, strategists met with the director of the program, and consultants from the public schools and universities provided input when needed. Figure 7.2 shows an organizational schema for the mobile-unit plan.

Administrators as well as teachers shared in the needs-assessment for the program. Administrators were a part of the decision-making body that determined the direction of the program and the way to implement it in the schools. Through the use of regularly scheduled task-force team meetings and frequent memorandum correspondence, area superintendents were kept informed and served as major input contributors to the program's objectives.

The project director worked closely with the coordinator of regular education. Major changes or additions to the existing program content or philosophy were discussed with all people concerned before they were implemented. The director of the program visited each team regularly during the week. The teams reported to the director's office daily concerning problems, attendance, and equipment and material needs. An agenda of Friday's meetings was sent to the strategists at their school locations. Any immediate communicating was done by phone or personal messenger.

Following are suggestions for implementing an effective mobile-unit organizational plan:

1. Set up a central committee to direct the program; however, all administrators in the program must be held responsible for implementing it.
2. Involve elementary school principals as active participants in leadership and follow-up roles.
3. Place emphasis on professional development for all; do not use the program merely for remedial training.

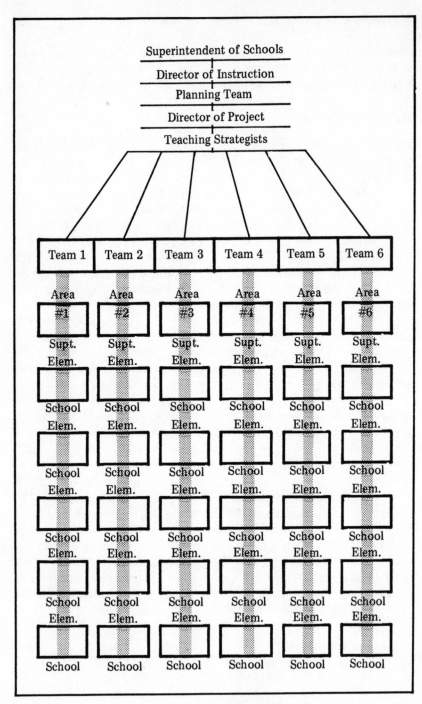

FIGURE 7.2 Organizational Schema For Mobile - Unit Plan

4. Include all teaching and administrative personnel as active participants in the program.
5. Place competent teachers who have demonstrated the objectives of the program in key schools to serve as modeling agents.
6. In each school, form a leadership team composed of key faculty members to share follow-up responsibilities with the principal.

Clinical Supervisor Plan

If supervisors are to become generalists as well as subject matter specialists, and if they hope to impact and implement strategies that actually change teachers' behavior in the classroom, then their supervisory roles and duties must change. The one-to-one, visitation-conference role must change to a clinical supervisory role. Clinical supervisors would be able to conduct laboratory sessions for large and small groups of teachers and would be able to videotape teachers' lessons to provide relevant feedback to the individual in light of a common set of objectives. They would be able to practice what they preach by modeling lessons that demonstrate program objectives. Then visitations and conferences would continue, but they would be one part of the program rather than the only part of the program.

Clinical supervisory techniques offer a number of advantages over traditional supervisory methods. Focus-on-the-learner strategies should be the domain of clinical supervisors for these reasons:

1. Supervisors are able to influence a greater number of teachers to a greater degree.
2. Supervisors and teachers work together as a team toward common objectives.
3. Supervisors become generalists as well as subject matter specialists.
4. The organizational format is designed to induce supervisors to believe in the strategies practiced.
5. Supervisors feel more worthy and have more prestige as clinical supervisors.
6. Teachers report positive feelings toward clinical supervisors and the programs they represent.

During the spring semester in 1972, supervisors in secondary education volunteered to engage in a focus-on-the-learner project that required them to attend ten laboratory sessions lasting 1½ hours each. (See Figure 7.3.) These were followed by four demonstrations lasting two hours, including discussion time. One junior high school and one senior high school were selected as laboratory sites for the project. Laboratory sessions were conducted at each site. Supervisors learned how to conduct sessions, operate videotaping equipment to tape teachers in the classroom, help teachers to see

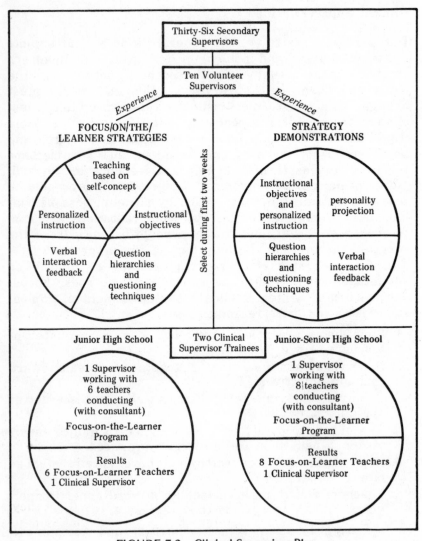

FIGURE 7.3   Clinical Supervisor Plan

themselves by using indirective feedback techniques, model lessons for teachers to demonstrate program objectives, and use effective visitation and conference techniques.

Then, supervisors working in teams selected a group of volunteer trainee teachers at each site and, with the help and direction of two consultants, implemented focus-on-the-learner strategies with teacher trainees in eight different subject matter areas, including foreign language and physical education.

OPERATIONAL FORMAT FOR FOCUS-ON-THE-LEARNER PROJECTS

Procedures and techniques for conducting all facets of the operational format are interrelated and supplemental, and all components are interrelated and based on a common philosophical base. Operational procedures are designed to attain focus-on-the-learner goals and objectives. Program participants meet competency criteria in all phases of the program at the same time because they experience each phase concurrently with all other phases.

Teaching according to a behavioral teaching plan was one strategy used to induce participants to look at themselves in terms of focus-on-the-learner concepts. Describing how this strategy works may help to clarify the operational format for the in-service center plan.

During *laboratory sessions*, participants received cognitive input by completing independent study modules, media modules, or seminar modules. When all participants had demonstrated competency in the cognitive domain, teams were formed for the purpose of writing and defending objectives based on student performance. The same teams then prepared and defended lesson plans that followed the behavioral lesson plan format. New social teams were formed, and each group chose a concept to teach to other participants not in their group. Each group planned and taught the lesson, operating on the basis of their behavioral teaching plan. Participants who served as learners filled out a feedback analysis chart,* which listed those things that helped or led toward completing or reaching the listed objectives, and they compiled another list of things that did not help them to

* See Appendix II for an example of a feedback analysis chart.

complete or to reach the listed objectives. Finally, individual participants viewed videotapes of teachers teaching students in regular classes and filled out the feedback chart. Consultants filled out feedback charts on these lessons, and seminar groups met with consultants for critiquing and discussion sessions.

Each morning, trainees were placed in regular classrooms where the classroom teacher was teaching using a behavioral lesson plan. As soon as the trainees were able to make out a behavioral plan, the *modeling operation* was initiated in the classroom. First, the master teacher planned and taught a twenty-minute lesson, and later, all three teachers critiqued and discussed the lesson in terms of the feedback chart. Master teachers had received in-depth training in interpersonal relations that enabled them to establish a positive relationship with participants.

As soon as satellite teachers were ready, they prepared and taught a twenty-minute lesson to students in their regular classrooms. These lessons were videotaped, and *feedback conferences* were conducted on a one-to-one basis with a consultant. Both the consultant and the trainee used the feedback analysis chart as an instrument for allowing the trainee to receive relevant feedback. The consultant attempted to build a positive self-concept while at the same time he provided valid data according to program objectives. Consultants *modeled, visited,* and *conferred* with participants when they were requested to do so by either the master teacher or the satellite teacher.

In summary, the operational format is composed of these interrelated components: laboratory sessions, regular classroom modeling operations, videotaping, videotaped lesson feedback conferences, and modeling, visitation, and individual conferences by consultants on request. The operational procedure allows participants to experience in-depth, focus-on-the-learner experiences that are tailored to help the individual participant attain program goals and objectives.

PROGRAM CONTENT (PHASE ONE)

The program content entitled Focus-on-the-Learner Strategies for Teachers (Phase One) was designed to allow teachers to analyze their teaching behavior in relation to focus-on-the-learner concepts according to their own beliefs and teaching styles. Each content area served as a separate instrument, while all topics were interrelated and supplemental. The program topics are depicted as a schema wheel with the initial topic beginning at the top of the wheel and proceeding clockwise around the wheel. (See Figure 7.4.)

Teaching Based on Self-Concept

Every moment of the day, during every teaching-learning act, teachers project personal attitudes and beliefs into classroom situations. Regardless of the words they actually speak, their verbal intonation and nonverbal behavior speak to students louder than words. Effective teachers must be skilled technicians, but they must be artists also. Strategies a particular teacher uses make up the technical component for teaching; the artistic component is made up of personality projections as observed by individual students.

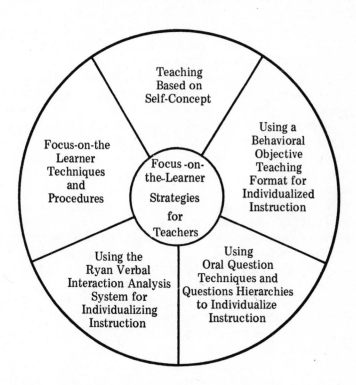

FIGURE 7.4 Program Topics of Phase One

Each student reads a teacher's personality projection from his own frame of reference. Generally speaking, teachers with positive self-concepts—that is, those who have positive feelings and beliefs about themselves that induce them to have positive feelings and beliefs toward students —can interact with students in the teaching-learning situation in a truly artistic fashion. Teachers with negative self-concepts—teachers who feel unliked, unwanted, unable, or unworthy—project these feelings into the classroom. Generally, students perceive this type of person as being a poor artist in teaching-learning situations, and the interaction process is thwarted.

The topic Teaching Based on Self-Concept was established on the hypothesis that people are born with certain potentialities or capacities, but their ability to fulfill their potential depends a great deal on their self-concept, which is often formed by stimuli they receive from their parents, siblings, peers, and other important people in their lives. When teachers are provided with in-depth interaction experiences with positive people, and concurrently they are experiencing success in all phases of an intensified program, the positive aspects of their personality are cultivated, and they become more positive personalities.

Focus-on-the-learner directors could not accept sensitivity training as the proper technique for inducing participants to look inward and to explore their feelings, beliefs, attitudes, and behaviors. Although the directors realized the sensitivity movement had been a pioneering force in the self-concept development field, unqualified directors using activities that were not educationally oriented or acceptable to teacher groups had caused many educators to view sensitivity training adversely.

Focus-on-the-learner programs allowed teachers to look inward and analyze their behavior by reading selected topics in the self-concept field and by engaging in peer-group interaction exercises that induced participants to test their attitudes and beliefs with others concerning a number of educationally oriented topics. These topics included motivation, discipline, role of a teacher in a democracy, indirective and directive methods in interpersonal relations, and teaching based on self-concept. Placing the emphasis on topics freed teachers to open up and to express their beliefs in a less threatening atmosphere than if they had been involved in exercises designed for the exposition of self per se. Self-concept behavior that demonstrated positive feelings was rewarded and reinforced by all members of the instructional team during all phases of the program.

Using Behavioral-Objective Teaching Format and Feedback Analysis Chart

During the decade 1960–70, the movement favoring the behavioral-objective teaching format descended like an avalanche on educators and affected teachers at every level of education. In some instances, writing behavioral objectives in precise terms became the goal instead of using objectives as a means to focus more clearly on student learning.

Focus-on-the-learner projects used the behavioral teaching plan to induce teachers to perceive their behaviors in terms of student learning. Teachers were required to measure entering behavior so that lessons would be valid for students. The plan also required teachers to be able to list those students who reached the objectives and those who did not.

Videotape operators focused the camera on student and teacher behavior; however, the major focus was on the learner. This procedure allowed participants to view their behavior in terms of learner participation and reaction. Keeping feedback analysis data on charts helped participants to analyze and to evaluate their procedures according to the teaching plan, which, in turn, was movement toward the overall goal—focus on the learner.

Using Question Hierarchies, Questioning Techniques, and Interaction Analysis Feedback as Focus-on-the-Learner Instruments

Question-hierarchy feedback and interaction feedback are compatible feedback systems that complement each other and the goals of the focus-on-the-learner program. While question hierarchies and questioning techniques focus on cognition in depth, oral interaction analysis feedback concentrates on the interaction process causing cognition in breadth. These feedback devices allow teachers to perceive their behavior with students without challenging the teachers' beliefs or teaching methodology.

Evidence, as shown on videotaped lessons, indicated that although teachers used questions often, little attention was given either to the purpose of questioning or to the proper techniques for questioning. Questioning techniques seemed to be structured according to chance instead of by design. To change that, the purpose for types of questioning and a study of question hierarchies were used as a basis for discussing questioning and the levels of thinking each type of question could stimulate in a student.

A simplified interaction analysis chart was designed that allowed participants to analyze their verbal behavior. The chart allowed them to observe that direct verbal interaction resulted in focusing on the teacher, as opposed to indirect verbal interaction that usually focused on the learner.

Teachers were able to chart interaction during a segment of class time. Results were tabulated, and participants could discern their interaction behaviors in relation to the teaching method, the subject matter, the capabilities and age level of students being taught, and the public school situation.

Interaction analysis became a part of the total self-assessment project, which allowed teachers to analyze their behavior in terms of concepts that focus on the learner. Interaction analysis procedures were simplified so that interaction feedback could be a focus-on-the-learner instrument that would induce teachers to use more indirective teaching techniques.

General Methods and Procedures that Focus on the Learner

Another instrument that allowed teachers to observe their actual behavior in relation to lip-service commitments that they espoused during laboratory sessions was an individualized instructional practices checklist.

Each group of participants constructed their own checklist by placing items under the following situational categories:

1. *The Classroom.* Items were constructed during laboratory sessions, where participants were divided into social groups of four members per group. Group members were asked to pretend that a teacher and students in their school had left the classroom for a play period. Participants pretended that they would inspect the vacant classroom and list a minimum of thirty-five things that would

be evidence to indicate that the teacher was individualizing.

2. *The Pupil.* Items were constructed under the pupil category as group members pretended that the teacher and students had returned to the classroom. Group members listed what the students might be doing during the remainder of the day that would be evidence that the teacher was individualizing.

3. *The Teacher.* Teacher methods and behaviors apart from student behaviors became checklist items as group members pretended that they were the teacher in the aforementioned classroom.

4. *The Lesson.* Group members listed general individualized lesson procedures, regardless of the teaching method, which would indicate that the lesson focused on the learner.

Items under each category were compiled, analyzed, and edited, and a formal checklist was constructed for each group member. This activity produced another feedback instrument that was related to, and supplemented by, all other focus-on-the-learner activities. Observing behavior in relation to an individualized instructional checklist provided participants with a culminating experience that motivated them to seek new and different methods for individualizing. When a majority of the participants exhibited an interest in change, the instructors considered the group ready for Phase Two. The entire program was usually in operation for about three weeks before the readiness signal became apparent.

PROGRAM CONTENT (PHASE TWO)

Once participants had received in-depth experiences in actual classroom situations designed to allow them to analyze their behavior in relation to focus-on-the-learner topics and instruments, a majority of them were willing to attempt a variety of methods and techniques that they might have rejected prior to experiencing Phase One of the project.

Of the participants completing Phase One successfully, only those participants who volunteered for Phase Two were selected to remain in the program. Careful screening of participants based on competencies exhibited during Phase One was also an important factor for recommending participants for Phase Two of the program.

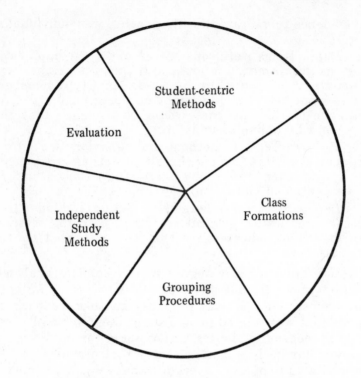

FIGURE 7.5 Program Topics of Phase Two

The organizational format and operational procedures for implementing Phase One of the program remained intact for Phase Two, but the goals changed. The goal of Phase Two was to provide teachers with new and different methods and strategies. Experiences for participants were designed to specify definite procedures for individualizing in a comprehensive manner.

Topics for Phase Two are depicted as a schema wheel with the initial topic beginning at the top of the wheel and the others proceeding clockwise around the wheel. (See Figure 7.5.) Specific instructions for implementing Phase Two became the nucleus for this book.

SUMMER WORK SESSIONS

A six-week block of time set aside during the summer for selected teachers and administrators to learn strategies for focusing on the learner can contribute toward an improved staff. In most instances, students are not available during the summer for in-service sessions. Although the absence of students lessens the effectiveness of the program slightly, the changed operational format includes a number of advantages for participants.

The regular program content and methodology for laboratory sessions are not changed for the summer program, but having participants on the scene full-time allows for program flexibility. Freedom from classroom responsibilities while attending sessions allows participants to concentrate on program content, and usually, some type of reward is given to participants for summer work sessions, which seems to make the program more enjoyable.

While the regular program involves teachers in teaching students videotaped mini lessons, videotaped lessons for the summer program involve participants in teaching peers. Role playing is not allowed; participants are required to preassess and teach content that is valid for peer learners. Warm, friendly, interpersonal relations among participants and session leaders should be developed during laboratory-session encounters before peer-teaching experiences begin. When administrators, supervisors, and teachers are included in the same group, group rapport, affection, and morale are affected positively if everyone participates in peer teaching on an equal basis. Demonstrating focus-on-the-learner competencies while teaching mini-lessons to peers has tremendous carryover value for administrative and supervisory personnel as well as classroom teachers.

Depending on group wishes, all participants may have feedback sessions for videotaped lessons as a whole group or each participant may receive individual feedback during a private viewing conference with the session leader. Frequently, summer-session participants request both private and group videotaped-lesson feedback sessions. Teaching a mini-lesson and receiving feedback according to preconceived competency requirements that are learned at the cognitive level during laboratory sessions is a program requirement. An essential part of learning to become a feedback agent is to experience personal feedback first as a teacher.

During the final phase of the summer work session, participants receive training as feedback agents. Videotaped mini-lessons of teachers who have formally consented that their tapes may be viewed at summer work sessions are used

for training purposes. Initially, participants view lessons together, and everyone helps to complete a composite feedback
analysis chart for Phase One of the program.* Later, each
participant views the same lesson and completes the analysis
chart for Phase One independently. After each participant
has completed the feedback data, participants compare and
discuss feedback items. The session leader views the lesson,
fills out an analysis chart, and serves as a discussion catalyst
for the group. Eventually, everyone is responsible for completing a feedback analysis chart and defending the items to
group members and the session leader.

Program participants must develop effective techniques as catalysts to encourage feedback on videotaped lessons. There are no set rules for interacting with teachers
while viewing videotaped lessons. Positive interpersonal relations are a prerequisite for success; therefore, many
interpersonal-experience exercises should be provided for
trainees. For these exercises, participants work in pairs. As
each pair views a tape of a teacher in a previous program, one
member plays the role of the teacher, while the other is the
feedback consultant. Depending on the maturity of group
members and the skills of the session leader, participants
may critique each other in a whole-group session or a pair of
participants may have a private feedback session with the
session leader. After each pair has experienced being a feedback agent, new pairs are formed, and the procedures are
repeated as many times as needed or as time will permit.

If summer-session work is to have strong carryover
value, a closely supervised follow-up program is necessary in
the fall. Administrative personnel should be responsible for
organizing and implementing a sound follow-up program in
their respective schools, and a resource person with a complete knowledge of the program should be available on a
continuing basis.

PRE-SEMESTER WORKSHOPS

Most schools reserve a block of time prior to the beginning of
the school term when all teachers are required to be available
for pre-semester workshops. This is an excellent time to involve classroom teachers and other members of the school
community in focus-on-the-learner sessions.

* Videotaped-Lesson-Feedback Analysis Chart, Appendix II.

After an interesting, concise description of the program is presented to the total faculty, small groups of twenty-five are formed for open question-and-answer sessions. Personnel who are interested in concepts that focus on the learner are asked to volunteer to spend their workshop time experiencing Phase One of the Focus-on-the-Learner Program.

Twenty-member faculty units are formed, and a project management team with a responsible coordinator is chosen to facilitate plans and evaluative procedures for the workshop sessions. Consultant services are usually available during pre-semester workshop time. A resource person with personal charisma, leadership abilities, and a thorough knowledge of focus-on-the-learner methodology may be selected to be the session leader, or a qualified person inside the school system may be selected. Much of the success of the workshop will depend on talents of the management team, the project coordinator, and the session leader. Special care in the selection of these key people is essential.

The workshop program requires eight laboratory sessions lasting two hours each. After each session, small groups view videotaped lessons of other teachers, who have consented to the use of their tapes in workshops. Laboratory sessions are activity oriented, and participants learn by participating in discovery activities. During videotape viewing, participants apply laboratory-session learning to a practical teaching situation.

The following content areas are the basis for workshop experiences:

Personality Projection and Teaching	(2 sessions)
Lesson Planning and Teaching Using a Behavioral Objective Teaching Plan	(2 sessions)
Oral Questioning Techniques and Questioning Hierarchies	(2 sessions)
Oral Interaction Feedback Analysis	(2 sessions)

Participant competencies are specified for laboratory sessions and videotape viewing periods. These competencies are stated in behavioral terminology so that accountability and evaluation is an integral part of the program. For example, one of the competencies participants must meet in the area of personality projection and teaching is to be able to list verbal and nonverbal behavior of teachers that led toward the attainment of stated behavioral objectives taught in a

mini-lesson. Participants are held accountable for accomplishing this competency during the laboratory sessions. During
the videotape viewing periods, they are held accountable for
accomplishing the competency at the application level.

Often, pre-semester workshops are conducted with
faculties, and excellent results are attained, but with the
beginning of the school term, carryover of workshop learning
into the actual teaching-learning situation is left to chance. If
strategies that focus on the learner are to become classroom
practices on a large scale, on-the-scene assistance and support are needed. Teachers are willing to engage in workshops
that deal directly with problems in their classrooms, but real
change takes place when professional growth projects are
conceptualized and implemented on the scene.

COMPETENCY-BASED TEACHER EDUCATION AS
A VEHICLE FOR IMPLEMENTING
FOCUS-ON-THE-LEARNER
STRATEGIES

Teacher preparation institutions of the past usually involved
students at undergraduate and graduate levels in course
work where they engaged in activities concentrating on talking and writing about teaching. Preservice teachers were
placed in field situations during student teaching where the
theory they had talked and written about in course work and
the practical classroom situations were sometimes poles
apart. Teachers returning to graduate education courses
were usually further confused when they engaged in course
work that did not apply to their school situation.

The movement for competency-based teacher education
is predicated on the thesis that teaching is a performance-
based profession. Proponents of competency-based teacher
education believe that teacher competencies can be stated in
behavioral terminology, and that students can be held accountable for demonstrating cognitive, performance, and consequence objectives at a predetermined level of competency.
The objectives and the competency levels are known by students and instructors as prerequisites for engaging in learning alternatives. Learning alternatives allow students to
travel different routes that are appropriate to their own
learning styles. Each chooses the learning activities that best
equip him to demonstrate objectives at the required compe-

tency level. Emphasis in competency-based education is on the learner. Instead of course requirements that focus on learning content in competition with others, students are held accountable for attaining a set of objectives, and assessment procedures and expectancy levels are known by the individual.

Competency-based teacher education requires a public school field component during each phase of the student's undergraduate and graduate preparation. Competency demonstrations culminate eventually in a public school setting. The movement for competency-based teacher education provides teacher preparatory institutions, the public schools, and the profession with a common vehicle for continuing education from preservice days to retirement.

There must be closer cooperation between teacher preparatory institutions and the public schools. Each arm of the profession must be willing to engage in team management operations. Compatible fields should be developed that meet the goals and objectives of the parties involved. Developing a clinical field situation for preservice teachers involves in-service teachers in worthwhile programs. When teachers completing graduate requirements at colleges and universities are involved in learning situations that culminate in the demonstration of competencies in their classrooms, then continuing education will replace in-service education.

Some focus-on-the-learner competencies are demonstrated during preservice education experiences. When the student demonstrates the competency in a compatible field setting, the field personnel must be a part of the teaching and assessment teams. Colleges of education and the public schools, as a cooperative enterprise, must provide education and training for public school personnel to complement the field setting. Once a clinical field situation has been established, it cannot be allowed to exist for more than three to five years, or else the school setting becomes a laboratory school. The goal for field experiences in undergraduate education is to develop clinical field situations, but not to allow the field situations to develop into laboratory schools. Each time the public school situation changes, a different group of public school personnel receives education and training. This operation constitutes a revolving system of continuing education for in-service and preservice teachers.

Competency-based graduate programs have a field component where objectives are demonstrated and competency levels are attained on the public school scene. Focus-on-the-learner strategies are part of many strategies that a graduate student should know and demonstrate. Instead of course work where experienced teachers talk and write about methodology, teachers demonstrate cognitive, performance, and consequence objectives in both the university and public school settings.

Inter-institutional staffing between public school personnel and university faculties is a desirable goal for competency-based teacher-education programs. Duties, responsibilities, and salaries should be shared by both institutions. If this type of team management operation becomes operational, then competency-based teacher education could become the vehicle for replacing in-service education with cooperative, continuing education.

PROGRAM EVALUATION

Focus-on-the-learner projects and programs have been evaluated on four different occasions. The two elementary projects were completed in different school systems, while the secondary projects were completed in the same school system.

Instruments and procedures for program evaluation included the following:

1. Pre- and post-project videotaped lessons of participants were evaluated in terms of program objectives. Teachers prepared and taught twenty-minute mini-lessons before the project began. On the basis of a program-objective rating scale, a jury of six educators evaluated the program by comparing the pretaped lessons with post-taped lessons taught after teachers had completed the project. Three jury members rated pre-tapes of a particular teacher before they rated the post-tapes, while the other three members reversed the procedure. The findings were positive in all cases; however, some teachers made much more progress toward the program objectives than others. Quite a few spectacular improvements were noted, so a program using pre-project and post-project lessons was constructed and presented.

2. Pre- and post-tests were given to students to measure educational gain. Standardized tests in subject matter areas were given to students in the projects on two occasions. In both cases, the results were positive; however,

there were situational variables in each case that cast doubt about the validity of findings concerning educational gain.

3. Participants filled out reports. Participants were asked to evaluate the project in relation to the program objectives. They filled out the forms anonymously after they had completed the project. Participants' reports were positive and included such remarks as "The first real in-service project that I have found to be really effective" and "Why have I not received this experience before now?"

4. Principals filled out reports. Principals evaluated teachers before and after they participated in the project, basing the evaluation on program objectives. Principals had received intensive training, and they were responsible for follow-up programs in their schools. They were required to evaluate teachers at the close of the school term according to the same objectives used in the focus-on-the-learner project.

   Reports at the end of the project and evaluations at the close of the school term were favorable, and positive results were reported in all cases. Of course, principals reported that some teachers made more progress than others. Teachers who were good teachers before they volunteered for the project made more progress than poor teachers. This finding caused administrators to implement the program on a continuing basis as a professional development program for everyone instead of using the program as a remedial effort for teachers having difficulties.

5. Average daily attendance records were kept on students involved in focus-on-the-learner projects. This attendance data was compared with average daily attendance records of students not involved in the project. Results showed that students in the focus-on-the-learner project attended school more often than did the students in the control groups.

The success of any professional development project depends to a large extent on the leadership of all members of the instructional staff. Not only must they be exceptional team members, but their skills in interpersonal relations must build self-confidence and enthusiasm in others. Careful selection of the instructional staff takes precedence over all other considerations.

While much has been attempted during recent years to meet individual needs by manipulating students, teachers, and curriculum, it is evident that no *administrative plan* can successfully eliminate the need for adapting instruction to individual differences within the classroom. It becomes the responsibility of the teacher to individualize instruction to meet innate differences in ability to accomplish scholastic tasks, differences in rate of achievement, differences in physical development and rate of growth, differences in personal and social adjustment, and differences in home background.

The techniques for class grouping and individualized instruction presented in this book are compatible components of a sound educational program.

Individualized instruction is worth the effort.

SUGGESTED READINGS

HARRIS, BEN M.; BESSENT, WAILAND; and MCINTYRE, KENNETH E. *In-Service Education: A Guide to Better Practice.* Englewood Cliffs, N.J.: Prentice-Hall, 1969.

HOUSTON, ROBERT W., and HOWSAM, ROBERT B., eds. *Competency-Based Teacher Education.* Chicago: Science Research Associates, 1972.

KARLIN, MURRIEL S., and BERGER, REGINA. *Experiential Learning: An Effective Teaching Program for Elementary Schools.* West Nyack, N.Y.: Parker Publishing Co., 1971.

LEWIS, JAMES JR. *Administering the Individualized Instruction Program.* West Nyack, New York: Parker Publishing Co., 1971.

MAGER, ROBERT FRANK. *Preparing Instructional Objectives.* San Francisco: Fearon Publishers, 1962.

MILLER, RICHARD I. *Evaluating Faculty Performance.* San Francisco: Jossey-Bass, Publishers, 1972.

———. *Perspectives on Educational Change.* New York: Appleton-Century-Crofts, 1967.

MOFFETT, JOHN CLIFTON. *In-Service Education for Teachers.* Washington, D.C.: The Center for Applied Research, 1963.

RUBIN, LEWIS J. *Improving In-Service Education.* Boston: Allyn and Bacon, 1971.

Appendix I.
Learner-Objective
Teaching-Plan Format

LEARNER-OBJECTIVE TEACHING-PLAN FORMAT

Teacher   **Date**

Lesson Topic and Instructional Goals

Pre-Assessment Procedures and Data

Learner Objectives

   Cognitive:

   Affective:

   Psycho-Motor:

Instructional Activities and Procedures

Listing of Materials and Equipment Needed

Evaluative Procedures

Percentage of Students Who Were Able to Accomplish Learner Objectives

Time of Lesson

Appendix II.
Videotaped-Lesson-
Feedback Analysis Chart

For Use in Phase One of the
Focus-on-the-Learner Program

INTRODUCTION

The Videotaped-Lesson-Feedback Analysis Chart is introduced during laboratory sessions, and participants receive
intensive training for using the chart as they learn to critique live and videotaped lessons. The chart serves as a
common reference umbrella for Phase One of the program.
Lesson planning and teaching using a Learner-Objective
Teaching-Plan Format permits the trainer to observe the
teaching-learning situation on the basis of what led the
learner toward stated objectives and what led him away from
the accomplishment of specified objectives. Because exercises
in personality projection and inter-personal relations are first
experiences for trainees during laboratory sessions, trainees
learn to critique lessons according to personality projection
before they concentrate on specific acts, questions and questioning techniques, and verbal interaction analysis. Eventually, they are able to critique a lesson in all of these
categories in one setting.

During laboratory sessions, small groups plan and
teach a mini-lesson to peers, using the Learner-Objective
Teaching-Plan Format. Learner participants begin to learn
how to use the Lesson-Feedback Analysis Chart as they
complete the sections of the chart that cover personality
projection and specific actions from the learner's frame of
reference. After small groups report on items that they have
placed on their respective charts, a group discussion is held
concerning differences in perceptions, with the session leader
serving as discussion catalyst. Later, trainees view videotaped mini-lessons and complete Feedback Analysis Charts

individually, as a prelude to a general discussion comparing individual lists.

As questions and questioning techniques and procedures for analyzing verbal-interaction feedback are learned in laboratory sessions, these categories are added to the chart, and the same training procedures are followed. Eventually, trainees are able to view a videotape of their own lessons and use the feedback-analysis information as a basis for conferences with the session leader, who has completed a feedback chart as preparation for the conference.

When trainee and leader use common reference points for which they both have received considerable training, much of the apprehension and fear that occurs when one observes one's teaching behaviors are lessened. Interpersonal relations between trainee and critiquer should be informal, friendly, and helpful. The critiquer's goal should be to help the trainee to perceive his behavior as factually as possible, while helping him to perceive himself positively as one who is improving. Depending on the relationship between critiquer and trainee, either indirective or directive counseling techniques are used by the critiquer.

The sample items listed on the depicted Videotaped-Lesson-Feedback Analysis Chart are typical items that appear as an observer watches many lessons. They are not sample items for any one particular lesson.

VIDEOTAPED-LESSON-FEEDBACK ANALYSIS CHART

Teacher Behavior That *Led Toward* the Accomplishment of Learner Objectives	Teacher Behavior That *Led Away* From the Accomplishment of Learner Objectives
Personality Projections	*Personality Projections*
Warm, friendly, enthusiastic eye-contact from teacher to a number of students	Does not look at students; has to refer to lesson plan often; eye contact dull, apathetic
Hand mannerisms match personality and help emphasize talk	Pulls ear; crosses and uncrosses legs
Sincere, open smile	Frozen smile; projects anger

Firm, well-modulated voice; enunciates clearly	Nasal, monotonous tone
	Uses threats
	Slouches, sits sloppily
Stands erect, but not stiff or reserved	Competes with students
Relaxed	Up-tight!
Sincere positive reinforcement	

Questions & Questioning Techniques	*Questions & Questioning Techniques*
Questioning technique and purpose for questioning coincide	Asks questions and then answers own question
Question level fits student's sophistication for answering	Uses more classroom-management questions than subject-matter questions
Gives students time to think before answering	Attacks students with questions
	Asks fact questions only
Leads students toward high-order questions	
Actual questions: 1. 2. 3. 4. 5.	Actual questions: 1. 2. 3. 4. 5.

Specific Actions	*Specific Actions*
Instructional model outstanding	Poor preparation
Walks among students during participation exercises	Tries to teach too many unrelated concepts
Uses concrete objects	Lesson too difficult for students
Channels lesson toward stated objectives	Does not know who learned and who did not

Evaluates at close of
lesson

Involves students in   Lack of student involvement
teaching-learning
situation

Holds students accountable   Passes out pictures and
attempts to lecture at the
same time

Verbal Interaction   *Verbal Interaction*

Amount of teacher-student   Practically all formal
talk varied and fits   lecture
purpose of the lesson
(indirect talk in   Students involved only
relation to direct talk)   as note takers
I.D. Ratio
indicates that students are
included in the teaching-
learning situation

Accepts students' ideas   Very direct and commanding
and feelings

Content teaching is evident   Rejects students' ideas
and feelings

Amount of teacher talk   Amount of teacher talk

_____   _____

I.D. Ratio _____   Student Responses _____
Student-Initiated Talk _____
Silence _____
Participation Time _____

Appendix III.
Comprehensive
Module Sample

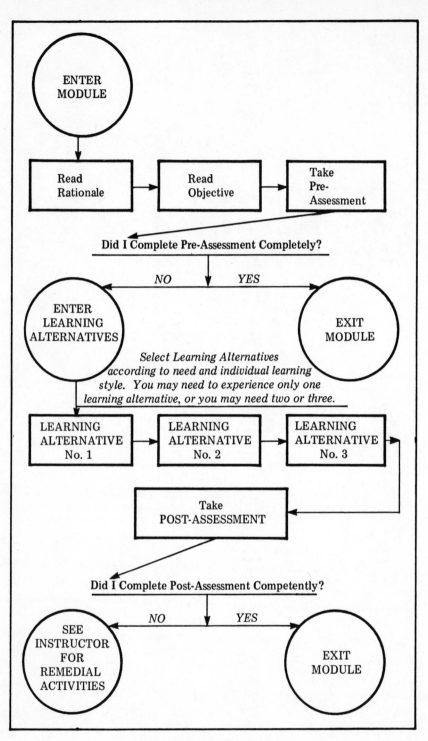

Steps For Completing Module

Reference System Designation: GEN-002.00 (HOU)

Program: The Sixth-Cycle Teacher Corps Program of the University of Houston and Houston Independent School District, Houston, Texas; the program is a two-year graduate internship for persons holding baccalaureate degrees in fields other than education; the program leads to a Master of Education degree and provisional certification; the program is focused on elementary school education, urban education, and the education of black and Chicano children.

Component: Generic Teaching Competencies

Module: Student-centric Teaching Methods

Developer: G. Ray Musgrave, Education Building 150, College of Education, University of Houston, Houston, Texas, 77004; 713-749-1010.

Date and State of Development: Summer, 1972; the module will be used for the first time during the fall of 1972.

Developer Comments: None.

User Comments: None.

GEN-002.00 (HOU): Student-centric Teaching Methods

Page 1

RATIONALE

If all students learned in precisely the same manner, if they all reacted to classroom situations in the same way, then teachers could select those teaching methods which best fit their individual tastes and personalities and use the same methods over and over again as long as they taught. Admittedly, this is the practice of many teachers; still, evidence clearly points to the fact that students have different learning styles. No two students react to a learning situation in the same way. Therefore, it is clearly evident that teachers need a variety of techniques that employ many strategies so that an individual student may experience that learning situation which best suits his particular learning style.

The predominant teaching methods that teachers still employ are teacher-centric; that is, the focus in the teacher-learner situation is centered on the teacher. For example, lectures and recitations are teacher-centric methods. Teachers need to be able to conduct teacher-centric presentations in an exemplary manner. Likewise, teachers need to be able to organize and conduct student-centric lessons in an exemplary manner. Examples of student-centric presentations are all types of discussions, panels, symposiums, sociodrama, and oral reporting.

This module is prepared to enable the intern to conduct student-centric teaching presentations effectively.

OBJECTIVES

1. The intern will describe acceptable methods for teaching the following student-centric teaching presentations: (a) small-group discussions, (b) large-group discussions, (c) panels and symposiums, (d) staged sociodrama, (e) whole-class sociodrama, and (f) discovery lessons.
2. The intern will select four of the above student-centric teaching methods and use them in conducting at least four lessons with elementary school children. The lessons should meet criteria developed by the intern's team.
3. The intern will evaluate his student-centric teaching presentations on the basis of student learning and acceptable criteria decided on by the intern's team.

PREREQUISITES

An intern should have demonstrated his ability to write instructional objectives and plan lessons before beginning this module.

PREASSESSMENT

The preassessment procedures consist of:
1. A pencil-and-paper test in which the intern is asked to describe the methods he would use to teach the following student-centric presentations: (a) small-group discussions, (b) large-group discussions, (c) panels and symposiums, (d) staged sociodramas, (e) whole-class sociodrama, and (f) discovery lessons. The test shall be administered and scored by the university instructor.
2. The planning, teaching, and evaluation of four lessons with elementary school children using each of four student-centric presentations. The adequacy of the plan, the teaching, and the evaluation shall be determined by the team leader, using criteria developed by the intern's team.

LEARNING ALTERNATIVES

The following are intended to assist the intern in meeting the objectives of this module:
1. During seminars, view videotaped lessons of teachers in the field using student-centric teaching methods. During and after the presentations, interns should analyze and critique the lessons. In addition, they should construct guidelines to be used in evaluating their own lessons.
2. After reading the resources listed below and attending discussion seminars concerning the readings, the intern will peer-teach, using student-centric teaching methods. The university instructor and interns will analyze and critique the lessons. Guidelines for evaluation

will be constructed for personal use. The following list of suggested readings should be helpful for these tasks:

BEYER, BARRY K. *Inquiry in the Social Studies Classroom.* Columbus, O.: Charles E. Merrill Publishing Co., 1971.

BOOCOCK, SARANES, and SCHILD, E. O. *Simulation Games in Learning.* Beverly Hills, Calif.: Sage Publications, 1968.

CARLSON, ELLIOT. *Learning through Games,* Washington, D.C.: Public Affairs Press, 1969.

CHESLER, MARK, and FOX, ROBERT. *Role Playing Methods in the Classroom.* Chicago: Science Research Associates, 1966.

GRAHAM, G. "Sociodrama as a Teaching Technique." *Social Studies,* 51: 257–59.

HEARN, EDELL M., and REDDICK, THOMAS. *Simulated Behavioral Teaching Situations.* Dubuque, Ia.: William C. Brown Co., 1971.

HOOVER, KENNETH H., and HOLLINGSWORTH, PAUL M. *A Handbook for Elementary School Teachers.* Boston: Allyn and Bacon, 1973.

HYMAN, RONALD T. *Ways of Teaching.* New York: J. B. Lippincott, Co., 1970.

KEYES, GEORGE E. "Creative Dramatics and the Slow Learner," *English Journal* 54: 80–84.

MORINE, HAROLD, and MORINE, GRETA. *Discovery: A Challenge to Teachers.* Englewood Cliffs, N. J.: Prentice-Hall, 1973.

STANFORD, GENE, and STANFORD, BARBARA. *Learning Discussion Skills through Games.* New York: Citation Press, 1969.

3. Participate as pupils as the university instructor uses student-centric teaching methods. Analyze and critique the lessons from both a learner's and a teacher's point of view.

POSTASSESSMENT

The postassessment procedures consist of:

1. A pencil-and-paper test in which the intern is asked to describe the methods he would use to teach the following student-centric presentations: (a) small-group discussions, (b) large-group discussions, (c) panels and symposiums, (d) staged sociodramas, (e) whole-class sociodramas, and (f) discovery lessons.

   The test shall be administered and scored by the university instructor.

2. The planning, teaching, and evaluation of four lessons with elementary school children using each of four student-centric presentations. The adequacy of the plan, the teaching, and the evaluation shall be determined by the team leader using criteria developed by the intern's team.

REMEDIATION

Remedial activities shall be designed by the intern and his team leader or university instructor as needed.

Appendix IV.
Specific Examples
of Individualized
Instructional Practices

MATERIALS

Activity centers

Balance between teacher-made materials and manufactured materials, charts, posters, bulletin boards . . .

Course outlines furnished advanced students who then proceed at their own individual pace

Interest centers in classroom

Student selection of reading materials with teacher's guidance

Variety of materials available to *all* students

Various levels of books being used in various subject areas

Various audio-visual aids readily available for students' and teacher's use

ORGANIZATION: TIME AND SPACE

Ability and achievement grouping within class

Flexible grouping of students for reinforcement of skills

Flexible program planning

Flexible room arrangement suited to instructional needs

Grouping based on testing program results

Independence and dependence grouping arrangements

Pupil self-direction; Pupil self-discipline

Student interest-grouping within class

Students with physical handicaps seated advantageously for needs

Time allowed pupil to pursue own interests

Teacher uses variety of methods for assessing students' abilities in relation to objectives and grouping

Use of coordinated programs

Varying time allotments to meet individual needs

INSTRUCTION

A variety of evaluation instruments and techniques are used in both pre- and post-assessment

Differentiated lesson plans and homework

Frequent teacher-pupil evaluation of behavior and work plans

Flexibility in class procedures to allow teachers to capitalize on unexpected learning situations

Individual assistance in and out of class

Individual encouragement

Individual evaluation

Individual files kept on each student within class, to which he contributes samples of his work regularly

Individual reports: oral and written

Learning activities are related to abilities, interests, and needs of children and whenever possible applied to out-of-school activities

Open-ended assignments

Problem-solving techniques used cooperatively by pupil and teacher in planning, solving problems, evaluating . . .

Providing real experiences: field trips, experiments . . .

Realistic challenges offered those students who desire to strive for higher achievement

System of individual evaluation in grading is used

Teacher and pupils cooperate in selecting problems and materials pertinent to the unit of work

Teacher asks more than tells

Teacher has genuine interest in pupil's background experiences to aid in learning situation

Teacher respects student initiative, uses consistency in planning, problem-solving . . .

Teacher-student participation in lesson planning

Teacher uses interest inventories

Tests structured to insure some measure of success for each student

Use of experience charts

Use of unit teaching; patterns in learning

Use of student experiences in classroom situations

Variety of Questioning Techniques used to draw on students' thinking and to develop related skills

INSTRUCTIONAL ACTIVITIES

As much (or more) student talk as teacher talk

Discussion in class using students' skills

Dramatization as form of creative expression, such as simulated television program

Individual and small-group projects

Much opportunity for self-expression provided

Media used as means of self-expression and communication

Private teacher-pupil and teacher-parent conferences

Opportunities for students to work in committees

Pupils encouraged to be self-evaluators

Pupil interaction encouraged

Sharing interests within class

Signs of students assisting one another

Small-group conferences

Small-group cohesiveness nurtured by teacher's interaction with groups; competition and collaboration among groups encouraged to provide choices and balance in interaction

Students plan ways to achieve goals

Index

DATE DUE

MAY 2 '78	APR 30 '78		
GAYLORD			PRINTED IN U.S.A

23-103